2

GHOSTS AT WAR

GHOSTS AT WAR

Paul Gater

CHIVERS

British Library Cataloguing in Publication Data available

This Large Print edition published by BBC Audiobooks Ltd, Bath, 2010.
Published by arrangement with Anecdotes Publishing.

U.K. Hardcover ISBN 978 1 408 49188 1
U.K. Softcover ISBN 978 1 408 49189 8

Printed and bound in Great Britain by
CPI Antony Rowe, Chippenham and Eastbourne

To Dilys

CONTENTS

INTRODUCTION

'Old soldiers never die. They just fade away'. So said the renowned American General Douglas J. MacArthur. But do the battle-scarred warriors—whether grizzled veterans or young privates or drummer-boys—really fade into oblivion? Evidence suggests that many are still around, lingering not only as individuals but particularly *en masse* on the sites of old battlefields. Shocked, traumatised, their spirits may feel trapped by fear and terror that continues to linger in places where battles were fought, not only in the First and Second World Wars but also from much, much further back in history.

It is commonly believed that ghosts are cold and remote. Veiled figures descending staircases, for example; an old monk walking through a solid wall, a child from another age still playing in some now neglected garden—these are a few of the more familiar images we think of when considering the ghostly realm—a realm widely known, imagined in clichés, yet in reality very little understood.

To begin with, exactly what is a ghost? Frederic W.H. Meyers, a founder of the Society of Psychical Research in London in 1882, described it as 'a manifestation of persistent personal energy, or as an indication

1

that some kind of force is being exercised after death that is in some way connected with a person previously known on earth'. Many people I have interviewed have encountered some sort of strange, inexplicable happening or sensation, whether or not they have believed in the supernatural; not necessarily by seeing a ghost but sensing, for example, strange, uneasy atmospheres or presences, when entering a building, garden or wood; or by picking up voices or unexpected sounds. That far-off hoot of an owl in the dark trees, could it really be a disembodied horn or trumpet-call? And is the more distant tap-tap the summons of a phantom drummer?

Amazingly, there are cases where people claim to have actually 'walked into' battles fought long ago purely by chance, finding themselves face-to-face with *invisible* combatants, being overwhelmed by the cacophony of jangling harnesses, thudding hooves of terrified horses, men shouting, the clash of swords or sound of gunfire, the agonised cries from the injured and dying. How *can* ghosts be cold and remote? The fact is, they are intensely passionate because they lived so passionately when alive, something that is often overlooked.

Areas of highly traumatic action in the past can still vibrate with echoes of the clash of arms. These were scenes of intense, emotional activity, extremes of bravery and determination, where everyone would have been fighting for his very survival in this life. Battles can still occupy places where acts of violence on a large scale occurred in an atmosphere of physical mutilation and death. Young men dying years before their time in large numbers, programmed to cling to their human condition until the last possible moment, could well have created a build-up of energy attempting to resist death, thus 'recording' their plight in a particular location.

Such energies, perhaps held in the fabric of buildings, terrain or even in the atmosphere, appear to be released or 'played back' during times when conditions are 'right', and are thus termed as being 'cyclic'. One particular example, so they say, happens at Cedar Creek in Virginia, USA, a location that has been described since October 1864 as 'one of the most haunted battlefields of the American Civil War'. Here, visitors unaware of the facts have picked up sounds of fierce conflict—musket-fire, canons, eerie bugle calls and cries from the severely wounded.

Another example is the Battle of Naseby, fought during the English Civil War near Market Harborough, Northamptonshire in 1645. What made this amazingly different to other skirmishes was that the whole event was seen in spectral replay in the sky for many years afterwards. Admittedly, there have been no repeat performances for some time now, but the living still feel they are being watched by long-dead soldiers, particularly after dark. Spectres of wounded Cavaliers and Roundheads have also been seen in the vicinity, dying under bushes.

And the soldiers have their own attending presences who still watch over them. Stranger than the ghosts of human beings are the legendary phantom black dogs that roam, supposed guardians of our ancient by-ways and wells, old burial sites and individual graves of the victims of *'dedes most fowell'*. Stories abound of witnesses who still encounter Roman soldiers in many parts of the United Kingdom—where Vikings too, it is claimed, have been sighted.

Why do ghosts or spirits linger after death? This is still a mystery, though there may be a variety of reasons why some find it difficult to pass on and others can apparently do so with ease. This is especially poignant if the ghosts occur as a result of battle, for throughout history, large numbers of people have been lumped together as 'the war-dead', lost generations who no longer exist within living memory, be they grasping Norman knight, drowned sailor or lone drummer or bag-piper.

Superficially, the ghostly realms may seem most easily accessible to storytellers, poets and artists. Some people have told me how much they would like to encounter ghosts, but cannot. Others do not seem to have any other option but to encounter spirits all the time in some hugely emotional, parallel universe, alongside that of the living. We are all psychic to a greater or lesser extent.

I assumed that my earliest encounters with 'the world of ghosts' were nothing more than an ever-growing collection of 'spooky' encounters, admittedly fascinating but unimportant. How wrong I was! My perception was educated over time to become aware that there can be immense significance in such meetings, and I now feel it is a privilege to be able to mingle in and salute that spirit world, parallel with our own.

There is a saying that 'While men fight, the women weep.' Perhaps that is the clue to why there are so many ghosts connected with war and battles. Let's face it, men like fighting each other. They always have. There are always those who do their best to stop wars— but there are always others who, if there were no causes for war, would very quickly invent some.

I would like to thank the many people who have shared with me their encounters with the supernatural, and have contributed so much to my research over time. I would especially extend thanks to my wife Dilys, an internationally-known writer and psychic, for her helpful comments and invaluable editorial skills during the preparation of this manuscript.

We walk strange paths that perhaps we may not altogether fully understand or want to examine too closely. But in this book, I would like to request the pleasure of your company as we go on a journey of investigation and exploration of the spirit realms, especially of the intriguing world of 'ghosts at war'.

Paul Gater

1
SOME VERY OLD GHOSTS

'And the air can turn even chillier at the sight of the still, staring figures of the MacDonalds.'

Anon

Imagine the scene. A ripening cornfield caught by the gentle ebb and flow of a summer breeze, the clear, crystal-sharp notes of a lark, high up in the blue sky . . . or the sun-drenched ruggedness of a Scottish glen . . . tumbling waters, in some picture-book setting that seems to offer us an opportunity to sit down and relax. Be careful, for such pastoral settings may not be all what they seem.

Why do we have a sudden sense of unease, a cold shiver down the spine, despite the heat of the day? It is because many such places hold strong feelings and can exude atmospheres of unease, tragedy, horror and intense sadness; we may be picking up echoes of some event, battle or massacre that occurred here on a large scale long ago, in early or recorded historical time—or sadly, even more recently.

In Scotland the name Glencoe (Gaelic for 'Valley of the Weeping') in Argyllshire, is a gruesome reminder of how entire areas of town and country may be 'active' from a supernatural point of view with the ancient passions, loyalties and betrayals of war. It was here, in February 1692, that a terrible massacre took place. On orders, some soldiers of the Clan Campbell first accepted generous hospitality from the MacDonalds then slaughtered them during the night while they slept. Spectral reminders of such collective butchery and cowardice still refuse to leave this remote glen and to this day, walkers in the area claim to have seen the ghostly forms of the murdered clansmen staggering about still traumatised by the event—particularly on 13th February, the anniversary of the atrocious act.

We might assume that moments of extremely high tension, particularly with regard to battles, acts of revenge and similar occurrences, are somehow preserved in the ground, atmosphere or in the actual fabric of buildings and can be released at certain times, so that the events can somehow be re-enacted. But how exactly would this work? Does the process require the build-up and then ebbing away of stored-up energy, rather like a battery? If not recharged, any battery will go 'flat', as they say, and perhaps this also occurs in the cases of ghostly encounters. It is on record that battles that were once seen vividly re-enacted in the sky over their original locations—such as the Battles of Marathon (490 BC), Edgehill (1642), and Naseby (1645)—have not been witnessed for some time now except, in the case of the latter two, for some paranormal activity still apparent on the 'sidelines'—soldiers at night seen dying in neighbouring fields and nearby woods. Even the highest levels of feeling and emotion will tend to drop eventually. And yet, strangely, it appears that some energy levels tend to last a lot longer than others.

Until recently, I was not aware of any ghostly sightings that pre-dated those of the Roman occupation of Britain. Then I came across information about what could arguably be called the country's 'oldest ghost'.

The figure is of a horseman from the Late Stone or Early Bronze Age, about 2,000 years ago, who is believed to be seen fairly regularly by people who live in the area as he emerges from a pinewood before galloping across Bottlebrush Down, North Dorset. He then rides alongside the A3081, between Sixpenny Handley and Cranborne. In the past the area must have been quite busy, although it is now fairly deserted. A Roman road from Badbury to Salisbury traverses the place and there are quite a number of low, burial mounds dotted around the vicinity.

The period in which the horseman must have lived was first identified in the 1920s by a local archaeologist R.C. Clay, by way of his dress—he was seen wearing just a long, loose cloak and brandishing what looked like a stone axe, or some kind of sword. His smallish horse had neither bridle nor stirrups. Mr Clay was returning home to Salisbury one evening from Christchurch where he was in charge of excavations at the site of a Bronze Age village nearby when, driving along, he first noticed the horseman riding at top speed across the fields towards the road. Sooner or later, he would collide with the car, so Mr Clay slowed down, thinking it was some local farmer's high-spirited son out 'on the loose'. The horseman, however, suddenly changed course, riding silently alongside the road for several seconds—long enough for him to be identified. Then rider and horse suddenly vanished by one of several ancient burial mounds in the vicinity.

Mr Clay never saw him again, despite several attempts to do so. But the spectral rider was seen on several other occasions, once by a group of local schoolgirls—again before vanishing by the same burial mound. Was he perhaps an early warrior? It certainly makes for intriguing thought.

The First Battle

Probably one of the earliest phantom battles seen occurred between Persian and Greek armies over the Marathon Plains. This was first witnessed shortly after the Greeks had proved victorious against what had seemed like overwhelming odds in 490 BC. Much had depended on the outcome—and though this might seem easy to say with hindsight, the Greeks were fully aware of the moment's significance at the time. Feelings had been running high, survival was paramount, defeat unthinkable.

Led by their courageous general Miltiades, with an army of possibly 11,000, his men were pitied against a Persian force of some 25,000 soldiers under the joint military leadership of Datis and Artaphernes—whose hands were nevertheless significantly tied by strict instructions from Xerxes, their 'King of kings'. The resulting victory went to the Greeks, but had they been defeated and lived under the despotic rule of the Persian king, they would obviously have been unable to develop their unique system of democracy. This would also have been lost to Rome and thence to modern Europe, and according to Tom Holland in his excellent book *Persian Fire* there would have been no 'West' as we know it today.

A Roman Soldier

'There he was! This Roman soldier sitting on a rock just several feet from us! He had a helmet, short sword and a sort of "skirt",' Vic

11

recalled, the excitement of the moment still ringing through his voice. 'We saw him when the morning mist suddenly melted as the sun came through, and just for a minute we thought it might be someone in fancy dress. But after about five seconds, it was like a light being switched off. He just disappeared!'

This unique experience was the climax of a recent walking holiday in the Lake District, undertaken by Vic and May, two early middle-aged outdoor stalwarts, in their mud-splattered waterproofs and heavy boots, who had agreed to be interviewed about their encounter with a Roman ghost, an event which had taken place somewhere, they said, between Pooley Bridge and Patterdale near Ullswater.

'Initially, we were flabbergasted,' May added. 'But when we'd had time to think about it, we both went all of a shake! Neither of us had seen a ghost before!'

For Vic and May, their innate psychic abilities could well have been activated by this encounter with the paranormal, widening their outlook on life at the same time. At all events, I felt that it had been a privilege to meet them.

The Roman Conquest

The Romans occupied Britain for a very long

time—from the 1st century AD, remaining here for approximately four hundred years. But perhaps their legacy was more than the physical remains of their stay—foundations of old buildings, substantial city walls, remnants of a road system, assorted artefacts—as well as the Latin origins of our language. Do their spirits linger too? It's certainly food for thought. Places like Chester and York teem with history, especially as they now promote their Roman 'legacies' as part of their very lucrative tourist industries.

I discovered that in various parts of the country such as Dorset, the Lake District and the Derbyshire Peak District, there are stories of Roman soldiers having been seen 'on the march'—places where they supposedly continue to tramp include over the hills of Purbeck and in Shropshire. From the ramparts of Burgh Castle, actually a Roman fortress, on the Norfolk coast, spectral legionnaires have also been seen keeping a watch over the North Sea for possible invaders.

With a commanding view over the beautiful Manifold Valley in Derbyshire, the cavern known as Thor's Cave has yielded evidence to suggest that man's occupation there goes back to very ancient times. It is also said to be haunted by a Roman soldier, left on sentry duty just inside the entrance. The George and Dragon Public House, along the Liverpool Road in Chester, is said to be built on the site of a Roman cemetery. Apparently that, too, is haunted by a Roman legionary who still believes he is on sentry duty. His footsteps have been heard going back and forth through the walls back and front of the building for many years. Likewise, two Roman soldiers— one of superior rank to the other—have been seen along the walkway on top of the famous city wall.

Another Roman soldier, of the X1 Legion, has been seen patrolling the amphitheatre and the tower foundations in Chester. Legend tells us that he was in love with a local girl, and would often desert his post to meet her. One night, he was ambushed by the Celts, and killed.

The Ancient Ram Inn, at Wotton-under-Edge in Gloucestershire, originally built in 1189 AD, is home to numerous hauntings. The original site is allegedly where Satanic practices were performed, ceremonial daggers having been dug up there alongside various bones. Intriguingly, one of the ghosts is that of a mounted Roman Centurion who rides straight through a wall. This was— understandably—much to the consternation of a plumber who was a witness on one occasion.

For years there was a local belief that a Roman centurion patrolled the Strood (a causeway linking Mersea Island to the Essex mainland), although it was not written down until the early 20th century by the Reverend

Sabine Baring-Gould. The figure was usually seen several times a year, particularly on 23rd September, at the start of the autumn equinox. There had also been sightings of other figures. The sound of clashing weaponry suggested they challenged the centurion, but Sabine-Gould suggested it was more likely that they had come to his aid against invaders.

Probably most famous were the Roman soldiers witnessed by young Harry Matindale in 1953, an apprentice working alone in the cellars under the Treasurer's House in the Cathedral city of York. I told the story in my earlier book *Living With Ghosts*. Briefly, he first heard what he thought was the sound of an old-fashioned claxon-horn. This was faint at first, gradually getting louder. Then, to his amazement and fear, a company of about sixteen Roman soldiers, headed by one on horseback, and blowing a crude kind of trumpet, suddenly came through the wall, slouched across the cellar and vanished into the one opposite. To his surprise, they seemed completely oblivious to his presence. Except when they walked across a freshly dug trench, Harry noticed they were visible only from the knees up, as though they were walking on some original level below the cellar floor.

He also noticed that they were dressed in the Roman soldier's normal short 'skirt' and leather helmets, their carrying long spears and short knives. The fact that they had round shields was to become a bone of contention.

Inevitably, the media tended to dismiss Harry's account as that of an imaginative teenager. Questioned also was his claim that the soldiers carried round shields. For several years, Harry refused to comment further, except to say that he had been telling the truth. It was not until several years later that a Roman road—the Via Decuma—was discovered under the foundations of the Treasurers' House. It was only when two archaeologists saw the company of Roman soldiers for themselves that subsequent research revealed that after the VI Legion left York during the 4th century, the auxiliaries who replaced them did indeed carry round shields. Obviously, their account had been more readily respected than that of Harry Martindale.

*　　　*　　　*

A sinister, solitary Roman soldier is said to guard a small stone bridge not far from Gwylfa Hiraethog, a ruined hunting lodge on the road crossing the Denbigh Moors (Mynydd Hiraethog), in North Wales. He has been known to materialise out of the mist, his plumed helmet easily seen, with a raised sword above his head. It has been suggested that he was killed by Celtic fighters during the Roman invasion—and according to Jane Pugh, author of *Welsh Ghosts, Demons and Poltergeists,* seeing him could have fatal results. Of two people who encountered him separately a few years ago, one died of a heart attack and the other was involved in a fatal accident soon afterwards.

Legends and strange sightings have certainly been the lot of ancient barrows and hill-forts set in the Purbeck Hills of Dorset. This has been particularly so since the 17th century, especially in regard to Flowers Barrow, near to Lulworth Castle. Phantom soldiers were first seen by Captain John Lawrence, a local squire, with some of his workmen. 'A vast number of armed men,' he recorded, 'several thousands, marching from Flowers Barrow, over Grange Hill.' This caused consternation, especially as the soldiers were thought to be real. The Captain and his work staff raised the alarm in the local villages and in nearby Wareham. All means of escape—roads and bridges—were blocked. Possibly, so they thought, this was part of a Popish plot. Lawrence also went to London to warn the Privy Council, but nothing further happened, so it was assumed the whole incident had been some sort of ghostly sighting.

As recently as 1935 the phantom army has again been seen and identified as Roman. It was noted that: 'On certain nights, a phantom Roman army marched along Bindon Hill to their camp on King's Hill; the thud of the tramping horses and men is plainly heard, and their indistinct forms seen as the fog drifts.' A year later, someone made mention of 'an army of skin-clad folk' descending from Flowers Barrow. Obviously this must have been some spectral sighting from much further back in time—perhaps akin to the early Bronze Age horseman of Bottle Brush Down.

Something more sinister happened during the autumn of 1891, when a young couple were making their way home from a fair at Llanrwst, North Wales. While walking near Lake Chwythlyn, a thick fog descended and they became lost so sheltered in a wood. Gradually, they became aware of strange sounds which at first appeared to be the effect of the wind; as these grew louder they heard the banging of drums, the clash of weapons, war-cries and screams of injured and dying horses and men, together with the sounds of high-speed chariots.

This supposed battle from long ago continued for almost an hour while the young couple cowered in terror, even though they could see nothing, not even vague shapes in the fog. Eventually, all went quiet again, the fog lifted and cold and shocked, the traumatised pair continued on their way home in the moonlight. They seemed to recover fairly quickly from their ordeal, and told their relatives and friends of their terrifying experience in graphic detail. But some months later, both their bodies were discovered in Lake Chwythlyn. Had the original event driven them to suicide? Or had their increasing curiosity prompted a return to the scene, where they had experienced something more horrific? A number of Roman artefacts have been discovered in the area for many years—did this unfortunate young couple stumble onto the secrets of a pitched battle fought long, long ago between Roman and Celtic warriors during the Roman Invasion?

More Welsh Ghosts

The annals of ghost-lore abound with stories of this kind. Two others, also set in Wales, don't necessarily have the traditional sad ending, but each is interestingly different. Neither, however, go back as far as any possible Roman 'activity'. Nant-y-Ffrith is a steeply-sided wooded valley, near to Wrexham and it was here, during September 1602, that chronicler Robert Barr witnessed an incredible vision. He wrote:

'. . . *was seane . . . in the edge of the eveninge to a number of 2 or 3 thousande armed men a hors backe with banners displaying in marchinge in warlike maner*

19

where as indeed there was no such thinge but some apparition of forewarninge of likelyhoode. And yet that was verefyed by 8 or ixen persons some of them credyte that all iontly saw the same.'

It seems that the 'forwarninge', or prophesy, never happened. No sightings of a physical army, let alone a spectral one, occurred later as far as is known. Maybe what Robert Barr saw was the ghost image of some long-forgotten medieval campaign.

In 1870, at Machynlleth in the County of Powys, a travelling preacher, Richard Rhys, stayed for the night at the house of the local deacon. Following a long day's journeying, he soon fell asleep in the comfortable bed provided, but was suddenly woken some hours later by the sound of a number of heavy footsteps coming up the stairs. The door burst open and in walked several men. The bright moonlight showed them as mostly rough-looking, dressed as soldiers from an age long gone.

Although the alarmed Rhys sat up in bed, the 'visitors' seemed totally unaware of his presence. Their leader sat down and the others did likewise, facing him. For a while they discussed various plans and ideas, then, as firm orders were issued, one of the men leaped forward, raising his sword at their leader, who leapt aside. Struggling with his would-be killer, the others clustered in a group. Then they all left just as swiftly as they had come into the room, their heavy footsteps fading into the distance, away from the house.

Rhys—as one might imagine—was highly disturbed at this invasion of his quiet sleep, and scrambling out of bed, he dashed to the window. But all was quiet. Not a soul was around. When he diffidently mentioned what he had witnessed to the deacon next morning, he was told that the house was certainly haunted—and by chance, a few years later, he was surprised to discover the original name of the building had been 'Parliament House'. According to an old legend: 'In 1402 Owen Glendower narrowly escaped being assassinated by Sir David Gain, the Fluellin of Shakepeare.' Had the episode been a re-enactment of that very incident, witnessed by Rhys, the travelling preacher, many years later?

Boudicca, Warrior Queen

Boudicca, the great warrior Queen of the Iceni has passed into history for her strong opposition to, and disastrous final battle with the Romans. She has occasionally been seen by some of the villagers at Cammeringham in Lincolnshire, appearing with her long, billowing hair flying as she stands upright, cracking her whip above the backs of the two horses pulling her chariot. Frantically driving at high speed from out of the early morning mist, the group makes its way along an old road the queen would have known on some desperate, though unknown errand of destiny. The wandering spirits of Bouddica and her two daughters have also been seen around the old earthworks at Ambresbury. It is alleged that they poisoned themselves here in order to avoid being captured in 62 AD, after the battle when the Roman Governor Suetonius Paulinus inflicted a crushing defeat on Boudicca's army.

No-one really knows the final resting-place of Boudicca. Some believe it could be under one of the main London railway stations or even Gop Cairn, near the North Welsh coast, the second largest prehistoric mound in Europe (the largest being Silbury Hill in Wiltshire). Excavations at the Gop, however, have shown that it is not a burial mound, its true function remaining unknown. It is, however, believed that Boudicca was a Druid, a member of the British priestly sect based on the island of Mona (Anglesey).

On her death, tradition has it that her body was secretly sent north, up through the Welsh Marches, to be buried on Mona's mystic isle. People living alongside the Old Route have occasionally heard the frantic galloping of horses and the grinding of phantom chariot wheels passing in the dead of night, bearing the mortal remains of the Warrior Queen, guarded by those faithful to the Druid beliefs. Discovering that Mona had been occupied by the Romans and the sacred groves destroyed, however, her loyal followers were forced to bury her on the mainland, possibly on the Gop, where a traditional connection with Boudicca has continued to persist down the centuries.

The religious sect to which she supposedly belonged seems to have been more of a male enclave. However, early Britons had a high regard for their queens, whom they would have regarded as 'earth-mothers' and Boudicca, a powerful priestess to her people, would have been held in awe. These are the facts that would have justified her body being taken on such a long and difficult journey for burial. Credence of a possible connection with Boudicca's final resting place in Wales happened one brightly-moonlit night in 1938 when a walker travelling from Diserth to Trelogan saw that a field below Gop Cairn was packed with Roman soldiers. Overseeing them on Gop Hill, with drawn sword, was a Roman general, a proud figure on a white horse. This incredible spectacle lasted just a few seconds until clouds blotted out the moonlight—and as far as I know, it has not been seen since.

Another well known 'haunt' is that of Bowes
Castle in County Durham. Hailing from the
twelfth century as one of Henry II's great
keeps, it is still felt to have a very powerful,
dominating presence all of its own, despite
being in ruins. Even more interestingly to us, it
was built on the site of a Roman fort. Legend
tells us that as the Roman occupation of
Britain drew to a close, discipline began to
break down and the garrison attacked the
surrounding area, looting and pilfering as
they went. Consequently, the locals banded
together and stormed the fort, massacring all
the soldiers in the hope of retrieving their
stolen property. However, in anticipation of
possible trouble, the canny Romans had
already hidden their ill-gotten cache, which
remains hidden to this day, despite the fact
that the legionnaires are said to be still seen
among the ruins of Henry II's castle, actually
engaged in burying the plunder.

Legend has it that about three hundred
years ago, a couple of local men spent the
supposed anniversary night of the massacre
among the ruins. Afterwards, they both
claimed having seen a group of phantom
Roman soldiers carrying a large chest of gold
and burying it. Unfortunately they were unable

to say where—and both died violent deaths soon afterwards. As a consequence of their efforts at treasure-hunting, perhaps?

In recent times there seem to have been many ramblers—besides Vic and May—who have experienced sightings of Roman soldiers—and I'm referring now to a whole spectral legion on the march, which is seen in full uniform with helmets and long shields, a thrilling sight as they pass carrying standards that fly in the wind. They have been witnessed crossing the bleak heights of the Derbyshire Peaks between Hope and Glossop, where there was an important military fort called Melandra (Ardotalia), built in the 70s AD and never reoccupied after the garrison left it around 140 AD. The ancient route followed by the Romans can still be traced through the deep heather and is believed to stretch back beyond Hope to what was the pivotal fort at Brough-on-Noe (Navio). This is now part of the Peak District National Park and although none of the local rangers have observed any such phenomena, they have certainly encountered the distress and shock of people who claim to have done so.

Into the Arena

The examples quoted so far have involved

people as merely 'passive' observers of some long-gone event. Although they tend to be more rare, there are also incidents known as 'Timeslips', 'Place Memories' or 'Immersion Timeslips'—on such occasions the observer, whether one person or several, can find themselves taken back to experience interaction between themselves and some long-past environment.

One very interesting account I investigated concerned Lord Percival Durand, who in 1829, together with friends, was sailing on the River Bure, close to Wroxham on the Norfolk Broads. Deciding to picnic on the bank, they disembarked from their yacht when they were immediately challenged by the sudden appearance of what they thought to be a dishevelled-looking old yokel who told them he was Flavius Mantus, Roman Custos for that area of Britain. He also informed them that they happened to be trespassing on Crown Land belonging to the Emperor Marcus Aurelius of the Western Empire, and that celebrations were due for His Majesty's birthday on that very day!

Naturally Durand and his friends thought they were dealing with a madman, or an eccentric to say the least. As they pointed out to the 'Custos', the Roman Empire hadn't existed for hundreds of years. But Flavius Mantus would have none of it. And before their eyes, he was suddenly transformed into none other than a splendidly presented Roman officer! Simultaneously, Durand and his friends found themselves among hundreds of spectators in a huge arena, all cheering and rising to their feet as a great procession entered, headed by standards flying and trumpets sounding. Then came many soldiers, followed by the golden chariot, drawn by a team of splendid white horses, of an eminent Roman general. He in turn was followed by lions led on golden chains. In complete contrast, hundreds of dusty, ragged, long-haired prisoners shackled together followed in the rear.

Then, much to the amazement of Lord Percival Durand and his friends, the vision faded. I discovered that incredibly, over a hundred years before (in 1709) the Reverend Thomas Penston, who was visiting the same area with his family from up North, had encountered the same crusty Roman Custos. Following an argument, he ordered the dumb-struck family to stand aside as the same procession approached, again with standards flying proudly and trumpets sounding.

At an even earlier date, on a summer's day in 1605, young Benjamin Curtis and two friends were swimming in the Great Broad at Wroxham. As far as I know they did not encounter the Custos, but the water inexplicably vanished and they found themselves dressed as Roman soldiers,

27

standing in that same arena on guard as the same phantom procession entered. When the apparition faded, the men calmly completed their swim before clambering back onto the bank, where they compared notes on what each had experienced.

This particular phenomenon is supposed to occur on a number of dates between the Roman Ides of March and the Nones of October. Emperor Marcus Aurelius must have had a lot of birthdays—and surprisingly close to each other! Historically though, he ruled from 161–180 AD. I discovered that a Roman arena was originally sited in the area, and that the procession in question would probably have come from Brancaster, a port on the edge of the Wash some forty miles North-West of Wroxham.

Although we shall encounter further examples of what we might call 'timeslips', they are best described as examples of quite phenomenal paranormal experience whereby someone who comes across a ghost (or ghosts) finds that the latter reacts to their presence. At the same time that person may find they are in a completely unfamiliar setting, or in one that they are familiar with but, somehow, in a different age. They have, as it were, wandered out of their own time and walked into another—the time of the ghosts they encounter.

2
SPOOKY SAXONS & VIKINGS

'. . . land and water
  ripp'd and bled;
  fire and slaughter
  —village dead.
  Now Robin Red-stain
  pipes a new September day,
  Recalling Eric Blood-axe
  Who once passed this wretched way.'

Fall
Anon

Even since the withdrawal of the Romans, there are certain events in particular that seem to have been indelibly imprinted upon the psyche of time. They are not necessarily all shot through with intrigue and bloodshed, as the quotation above might suggest, although the more dramatic do appear to leave an amazingly powerful impression.

It is said that on July 21st, every five years, the spectral coronation of King Ella, an early Anglian king, is re-enacted by the spirit of the Lord Abbot of Norwich. This takes place at Horning by the River Bure, roughly one hundred yards downstream of the Swan Inn, a hostelry named after Ella, who became known as the Swan of Peace. The actual crowning dates back to shortly after the Roman withdrawal from Britain at the start of the 5th century AD. The reason why this particular event has been 'preserved' remains, however, a baffling mystery. Maybe the good Lord Abbot (or the king himself, in spite of his peaceful image) was a man with a large ego!

A more familiar name—that of Arthur, 'the boy born to be king', according to T.H. White, author of *The Sword in the Stone*—has given rise to a multitude of ghostly Arthurian legends which have evolved over time. Although believed to have been a British chieftain who lived around 500 AD, Arthur is more usually represented as a brave, medieval-type warrior of the Age of Chivalry, surrounded by knights in shining armour. We love to believe in this image, even though the Age of Chivalry was established by Edward III in the 14th century, almost a thousand years later. But whoever he was, whatever he looked like, Arthur must have been a remarkable man to score so valiantly against the Saxons who swarmed to invade British shores after the Romans had departed. He became the icon of the perfect monarch, legends portraying him as still in an enchanted sleep, waiting to arise if needed, England's saviour in 'once and future' times of stress and danger—if not in person, then certainly in spirit.

It is believed that Arthur's ghost haunts

Cadbury Castle in Somerset—the most likely site of his court of Camelot, perhaps, though there are several places which claim this honour. On Midsummer's Eve, a mysterious form is said to lead a company of loyal followers along a causeway not far from the castle while on winter nights, amid the sounds of barking dogs and shouts from his men, 'Spectral Arthur' has been seen taking everyone out on a hunting expedition. During the 19th century, it was said that his hunting horns were heard over the moors around Castle-an-Dinas in Cornwall, and he is also reputed to appear at the famous Tintagel Castle, also in Cornwall. This is his supposed birthplace while Glastonbury, assumed to be the legendary Isle of Avalon, is where he is buried alongside his queen, Guinevere.

Phantom Saints

An old, but true story may become embroidered over several hundred years, each generation adding or taking something of the fact away, then reassembling the remaining pieces so that what remains might be surprisingly different to the original. Consecrated in 1124, the church at Castor, near Peterborough is the only religious establishment in Britain dedicated to St.

Kyneburgha (later known as St. Cyneburg). She was one of many Anglo-Saxon royal saints, her father believed to be Penda, King of Mercia (died 654 AD). She was married to Alcfrith, son of King Oswin of Northumberland.

Later, Kyneburgha became a Benedictine nun and in about 650 AD, founded a convent with her sister St. Cyneswith and St. Tibba, another relative. St. Cyneburg died around 680 AD and was buried in the Church at Castor, as were the other women. Their remains were in due course moved by Abbot Aelfsige of Peterborough (died 1042) to Peterborough Abbey where they were venerated: in time they were moved to Thorney, but returned to Peterborough in the reign of Henry I (1100–35).

So much for the background. The town of Castor once had a number of ruined Roman buildings, through which ran a track that the people chose to connect with their well-loved saint, who had, according to popular legend, performed some miraculous act or acts there. In 1712 (by which time the track had become known as Kinnesburga's Way in a further corruption of the saint's name) the Revd. John Morton described it as being narrow and barren, heading out to the more lush areas beyond. He recounted in his writings how she was once pursued by a gang of scoundrels as she ran through the fields—one tradition says

32

that the contents of her basket spilled out onto the ground and turned into bushes that waylaid her would-be attackers. Another states that as the desperate woman stumbled to save herself, the way 'unrolled itself before her as she fled'.

Round about the same time, a William Stukeley recorded in his diary the events of a visit he had paid to Castor. He noted that the town still had a monument to the saint and maintained a tradition that she had been seen travelling along the Roman track in a coach and six 'some few nights before Michaelmas'. Stukeley referred later to the abbess and her nuns as having been murdered by the Vikings. He interpreted the tradition of the saint and her phantom coach as perhaps arising from the corporate fading memory of her festival, which had been celebrated at Castor until the Abbot of Peterborough removed her mortal remains, on 15th September, the anniversary of her death.

Slightly later from these disputed years of conquest and counter-conquest, is the disproving ghost of Editha, grand-daughter of Alfred the Great. Known as the Black Lady (for good reason) she still haunts the steps that lead up to the Tower Room of the castle at Tamworth in Staffordshire, a town originating in Saxon times, which was once the capital of the Anglo-Saxon kingdom of Mercia, in the reign of Offa. Wearing a black habit, Editha and her sister Benedictine nuns were expelled from their abbey at nearby Polesworth when Tamworth was granted by William the Conqueror to Baron Roger de Marmion as a reward for his loyalty, following the battle at Hastings in 1066.

A later Lord de Marmion found himself challenged by Editha's fearsome spectre, which warned him of impending death if their abbey at Polesworth and its lands were not returned to the Benedictine nuns. She actually struck him with her staff, causing an injury which never completely healed over the ensuing months—giving him time to consider the matter—until at length, he agreed with great reluctance to the spectre's request and his injury, as if by magic, was subsequently healed.

Knights and Ladies

Tamworth Castle is also haunted by a heartbroken White Lady from an earlier period, who wanders in tears, high on the battlements. Her lover, Sir Tarquin, was a Saxon knight killed in a duel with Sir Lancelot, one of King Arthur's knights, which was fought on Lady's Meadow, below the castle walls.

Seen in the park of Ragley Hall, Warwickshire is another White Lady who sits on a certain stile before going down to a nearby stream to drink. It is interesting to note that in ghostly lore there have been long associations between White Ladies with regard to water, gates and styles. Where this particular one comes from no-one seems to know, although she might be connected with the discovery in 1833 of the skeleton of a woman in an ancient grave. Artefacts buried with her, including brooches and a dagger, suggest she might have been from Anglo-Saxon times.

Back at Tamworth Castle, Baron Roger de Marmion wasn't the only 'loyal buddy' to be rewarded by the Conqueror. Another was Henry de Ferrers—Tutbury Castle, also in Staffordshire, becoming one of his prizes through victory. This became noted much later as one of the many places where Mary, Queen of Scots was imprisoned, but by 1977 the Castle belonged to Barry Vallens, originally from Derbyshire, who encountered several ghosts, including that of a monk in a brown habit and a lady in white. Probably the most challenging presence was that of a Norman knight, possibly one of the original de Ferrers, whose tomb was in the ruins of the chapel of the Castle. It was in there that Mr Vallens discovered an ivory and silver ring which he decided to take home and clean.

It does not appear that the phantom Norman knight, as such, was ever seen, although Mr Vallens and his wife experienced a disembodied hand knocking on one of the windows and things crashing and thudding during the night, though investigation the next morning revealed no actual damage. Deciding that the portents seemed ominous, however, the Vallens acted wisely. The ring was returned to the old chapel, and the restless knight was restless no more.

A restless spirit which may haunt for ever more has been seen at Chanctonbury Ring, situated high on a ridge of the South Downs, near to the village of Washington. 'Ring' was the original name of a small, Iron Age hill-fort which is now barely conspicuous. In 1760, sixteen-year-old Charles Goring, a member of the local gentry who owned the site, planted a thick clump of beech-trees and as they matured, they became known as the Chanctonbury Ring, rather than the hill-fort, and became in more recent times a favourite place for walkers and outdoor family activities.

Nonetheless, because of its obvious connections with the ancient hill-fort, the site accumulated many legends. Equestrian types said their horses were reluctant to go near the trees, possibly because there were phantom horses around; even a spectral lady on a white horse. There is also the ghost of a white-bearded Saxon who was killed at the Battle of Hastings. On his way there, he reputedly buried some treasure and, to this day, he wanders round and round the Chanctonbury Ring hoping to recover it.

Strange and Terrible

The intriguing thing about supernatural encounters is that no-one knows what form they may take or when they might happen. Often, it is purely by chance that we may experience them for even 'anniversary' ghosts cannot always be relied upon for their punctuality. Even if a presence is not visible—and the majority may not be—our senses can instinctively pick up something in the atmosphere—there are phantom smells, say, of cigar or cigarette smoke, beautiful scents, perfumes and aromas—or revolting ones! There may be sounds—voices, laughing, crying—screams, for example. Or we may be aware of unseen movement—or simply that familiar 'atmosphere', whether 'spooky' or not.

Even the least psychic among us are surely aware of having arrived, say, at a friend's house where there has just been a row—and you can feel it in the air. If just a 'one off', the atmosphere in the house soon returns to an accepted normality, but in places where rows and bust-ups are the norm, a dark build-up of negativity can occur, which may encourage other negative entities to move in. If we imagine this on a much larger scale—on say, some ancient battlefield—we can see how the ghostly presence can continue to feed on itself. Although even in the worst places, there is always hope.

I came across such a case set in the North-east of Scotland. Miss E. Smith, a middle-aged woman, was driving home from Brechin to Letham one snowy January night in 1950. As a result of the bad weather, her car skidded in an isolated area, ending up in a ditch. In an era long before mobile phones, she had no way of calling for help and decided to walk the few remaining miles to her destination. Approaching Letham she caught sight of distant flaming torches moving around in the dark near Dunnichen Hill, and on drawing closer she noticed men—strangely-dressed in coarse brown tunics and leggings—wandering around, eyes lowered. They seemed to be searching for the bodies of other men which Miss Smith could see were lying on the ground; no-one, strangely, paid any heed to her presence.

During the late 7th century AD, it is known that the Battle of Nechtanesemere took place between the Northumbrians and the Picts, on a site near Dunnichen Hill in Angus. Led by Brude mac Bile, the Picts were to heavily defeat the Northumbrians, even killing their King Ecgfrith. This was the blow that finally ended any Northumbrian ambitions to move further north and it would seem that Miss Smith had actually witnessed the spectral survivors of the battle still searching for their dead and injured comrades, in the hope that the terrible disasters of the day might at last be healed.

Another blood-curdling story concerns three kings who met at Dacre Castle in 926 AD. They were the Saxon King Athelstan, Owain of Cumbria and Constantine of Scotland who, in an effort to lay low their bloodlust for each other, sat down determined to talk of peace. The sad results, however, were greater and more bloody battles, terminating at Brunanburgh with the slaughter of many hundreds of Saxons. But guess what! After more than a thousand years the ghosts of these three 'wise' kings still haunt Dacre Castle—increasingly desperate to resolve their many differences, perhaps?

An equally indelible drama of about the same period is said to replay itself in the town of Shaftsbury, in Dorset. Two spectral men have been witnessed leading pack-horses up Gold Hill. They are transporting the body of Edward, the 18-year-old heir to the Anglo-Saxon Throne, who had been ruthlessly killed by his stepmother, Queen Elfrida in Corfe Castle, so that her own son would be in direct line: the phantoms are on their way up to the abbey where Edward is to be buried. All kinds of miracles are believed to have happened during that final journey back to Shaftsbury, which was where the luckless prince became enshrined as St Edward, the Martyr. Subsequently, Queen Elfrida's son became known as Ethelred the Unready.

Viking Ghosts

More information I researched concerned alleged sightings of Viking soldiers. One, located on Canvey Island, Essex, is the phantom of a fierce-looking, six-foot tall man with long moustaches and beard, complete with a horned helmet, belted coarse leather jerkin and narrow lengths of similar material wound round his legs. Armed with a long sword, fishermen have seen him wading out of the sea to cross the mudflats at Canvey Point. He is believed to have been part of an invading horde led by Halvdan, who was defeated by Edward the Elder, a son of King Alfred the Great, in 894 AD.

Going one step further, the 17th century Prospect Inn at Exeter, a much haunted public house situated on the bank of the River Exe, has an historic—and also haunted—quay. A phantom Viking longboat has been seen travelling up the river, heading towards the quay with a wild-looking, long-haired warrior standing in the bow, waving his fist in a threatening manner.

Attacked In a Haunted Church

'Falling . . . on my back, one of them stood over me, his face laughing with triumph as, holding his sword in both hands, he drove it into my chest.'

Maurice Cottham, writing in
Psychic News

The atmosphere of many recognised religious sites can be extremely powerful even if the buildings are in ruins or even non-existent now. Many of our older Christian churches and abbeys were built on former sites of Celtic religious practice, areas with strong, positive energy fields, possibly ley-line intersections. Where a positive ley-line comes into contact with a negative influence then it, too, will become negative, thus attracting negative spirits—sometimes though, there can be a mixture of positive and negative, according to a number of reasons.

The Spiritualist newspaper *Psychic News* reported some fascinating experiences of Maurice W. Cottham, a guide at St Peter's Church in Monkwearmouth, in the North-east of England—a building that is all that remains

41

of what was the most important Saxon monastery in the whole of Europe. Maurice Cottham had been psychic since childhood, and this was where he claimed to have seen more ghosts than in any other location –actually experiencing something incredible almost every time he entered the place. Several times he found the church full of Saxon farmers and fishermen, accompanied by their families, all wearing sheepskins and woollen clothing and seated on rough-hewn benches. Children were running around everywhere. There was noise, life, a sense of happiness and holiday. Amid the cacophony, a couple of monks were holding service in an atmosphere strong with the smell of incense.

On another occasion, in complete contrast, Maurice reported that he entered alone, and this time the light within was strangely dim. He knew the building had been ransacked once by the Vikings and then again by the Scots. He must have felt somewhat apprehensive on his own with the place now dark and deserted. Suddenly, an outside door burst open and in charged a group of armed men dressed in similar clothes to the Saxon church-goers. As Maurice tried to stand in their way he was immediately struck down onto his back. He looked up into the leering face of a brigand who, with both hands, drove a sword straight into his chest. Maurice reported feeling agonising pain as the weapon went home. The next thing he remembered was standing in the Church again, severely shaken but alone with all sign of the invaders gone. He was of course unable to identify his attackers, but wondered if he had re-lived some terrible experience that had lingered there, perhaps concerning one of the monks who had perished on that very spot during such a raid.

Viking Wrath and Slaughter

Hardly any part of Britain was immune from the savagery of the Vikings. Their long-boats, designed to cover great distances over seas, could also navigate the much shallower waters of rivers and penetrate into areas that were situated comparatively inland. Islands around the coast were of course even more vulnerable, and one of the earliest attacks which occurred in 793 AD was thus recorded in the Anglo-Saxon Chronicle:

'Terrible portents appeared in Northumbria, and miserably inflicted the inhabitants; there were exceptional flashes of lightning and fiery dragons were seen flying in the air, and soon followed a great famine, and after that in the same year the harrying of the heathen miserably destroyed God's church in Lindisfarne by rapine and slaughter.'

Situated in woodland on the Kyloe Hills is a place known locally as Cuddie's Cave (Northumbrian for St. Cuthbert's Cave). It was here, according to legend, that the saint's coffin was concealed by fleeing monks when Lindisfarne was attacked by the Vikings. As Bishop of Lindisfarne he had often taken shelter in the cave and sometimes spent the night when visiting various parts of his scattered diocese. Although probably not haunted by St. Cuthbert's spirit, the area is said to host the phantom of 'Hazelrigg Dunne', killed as a common thief several centuries later. Though seen in human form, this character was apparently a 'shape-shifter' who could also make himself visible both as a wild horse and a donkey.

Another letter published in *Psychic News* was written by Derrick Waters of Doncaster, who shared with readers two incredible accounts of his own somewhat alarming 'brushes' with Vikings. The first took place in 1966, when he and his wife were travelling by car along the B1205 near Kirton Lindsey, North Lincolnshire. He began to feel aware of a pressure of gloom and looking up, noticed that the sky, on that hot summer afternoon, was suddenly darkening as though for a thunderstorm.

Pulling over on to the grass verge, he felt a great sense of foreboding and on getting out of the car, he saw a band of savage Vikings crossing a nearby field heading in his direction. Despite being visible only from the waist up, he noticed they were armed and seemed acutely threatening. He was about to jump back into the car for a quick getaway, when they faded within thirty to forty yards of the vehicle.

His wife had not been aware of any darkening of the sky or seen any Vikings, and was completely puzzled by Derrick's behaviour. Obviously they had been in different dimensions during that short period, the probability being that Derek was more acutely psychic and able to 'pick up' things more readily.

Where spectres are only seen minus their lower regions the suggestion is that the level of an existing floor, road, or terrain was lower when they were there physically—though an alternate school of thought suggests that it could be due to diminishing energies in the ley lines.

Derrick's second encounter occurred some thirty years later. This time he was driving about fifteen miles west of Bridgnorth, Shropshire and had turned onto the A49, heading north to Shrewsbury. Forced to slow down, he suddenly and much to his amazement, found himself in the midst of a battle in which Vikings were involved. He reported that he maintained a slow speed for about two hundred yards, feeling far less threatened than on the first occasion, and then suddenly saw them disappear. He later learned he had been close to the famous ancient hill fort of Caer Caradoc and wondered if, perhaps, the local inhabitants had reoccupied the place after the Romans left Britain, and were in due course attacked in later centuries by the Vikings.

Derrick felt sure that what he had experienced were time slips, and recalling those well-documented Roman encounters close to Wroxham, on the Norfolk Broads, one wonders whether those spectral Vikings—especially on the occasion of the first sighting—actually saw him and his car. What might they have thought of that piece of horseless 20th century wizardry? It could be possible that they in their turn were terrified by a vision inducing feelings *we* might experience on encountering a genuine spacecraft from some other galaxy!

3

CIVIL WAR GHOSTS—ADVANCE!

'Between twelve and one o'clock in the morning was heard by some sheepherds, and other country-men, and travellers, first the sound of drummes afar off, and the noyse of souldiers, as it were, giving out their last groanes: at which they were much amazed . . . But then, on the sudden . . . appearing in the ayre those same incorporeall souldiers that made those clamours, and immediately, with Ensignes display'd Drummes beating, Musquets going off, Cannons discharged, horses neyghing (which also to these men were visible), the alarum or entrance to this game of death was struck up . . . Till two or three in the morning, in the equal scale continued this dreadful fight . . . so amazing and terrifying the poor men, that they could not give credit to their ears and eyes; run away they durst not, for feare of being made easy prey to these infernal souldiers, and so they, with much feare and affright, stayed to behold the outcome of the business.'

A Great Wonder in Heaven
17th Century Pamphlet

This was no revelatory description of the Seven Horsemen of the Apocalypse, but an account of a vision of the Battle of Edgehill (Warwickshire), fought on 23rd October 1642 and notorious as the first major encounter of the English Civil War. Intriguingly, the pamphlet describes how, during several nights over the Christmas period following, opposing spectral armies were heard and seen in the sky over the original battle site.

Many people were witness to the spectacle of the entire grim drama being re-enacted, finishing with the defeat of the Royalists. Indeed, word reached King Charles I at Oxford, who as we might imagine, was rather disturbed and sent his personal representatives to investigate. They not only took sworn statements from witnesses, but ended up seeing the vision themselves. It is actually recorded that some of those who had been engaged in the original battle saw themselves appearing in the ghostly re-enactment, and they were able to identify individual friends and foes who they knew had perished at Edgehill.

Although the full drama of this spectral vision has not been experienced for some years (the supporting energies having 'run out' perhaps?) it was seen as recently as the 1970s, when people in the area claimed to have seen the 'replay' on the anniversary of the battle—

23rd October. Though he survived the slaughter the ghost of Prince Rupert, the King's nephew, has been seen on the battlefield itself and so has that of Sir Edmund Verney, the Royalist Standard Bearer (who did not survive, as we shall discover). More recently visitors to the site at night have felt they were being watched by long-dead soldiers, and there have been accounts of witnesses seeing dying Royalist and Roundhead officers collapsed and gasping their last under the shelter of bushes. Surprisingly—or not, as the case may be—the same occurrences have been reported following another Civil War encounter, the decisive Battle of Naseby in 1645.

*   *   *

Briefly the Civil War Period (1642–1651) was a desperate struggle for power between Charles I and his followers (members of the Establishment Anglican religion) and those who opposed him in Parliament, mainly the Puritans. The King, with the support of a few hand-picked ministers, had ruled absolute, passing his own laws which increasingly showed that he was mostly out-of-touch with everyday reality. The House of Lords, consisting of influential noblemen, held some sort of power but that of the Commons had almost no say in terms of real government.

Peopled as it was by landed gentry and members of the middle classes, they were disturbed, then furious to discover to their cost that to oppose the King's legislation meant heavy fines, confiscation of property and other threats of royal disfavour.

There was mounting opposition against the Royal Absolutism and inevitably, things came to a head. Charles, however, was a man who vacillated when it came to making important decisions, or else rushed in on impulse, with no forethought as to the consequences—and it was this flaw which would in the end cost him his throne and his life.

Through a whole series of constitutional crises, the people's loyalty to the Crown had been sorely tested since his accession in 1625, and it was John Hampton and John Pym, together with other members of the House of Commons, who took the first stand against the King, openly refusing to accept any more royal impositions. On 4th January 1642 Charles defiantly entered the Chamber, demanding the surrender of five members whom he considered the leading trouble-makers— however, very prudently, the gentlemen in question were not present. But all patience was running out and both King and Parliament knew that open conflict was inevitable, though it was not until eight months later that Charles finally raised his colours at Nottingham and war was declared.

The Civil war set brother against brother, cousin against cousin, opposing loyalties, alas, splitting many once-united families—fathers even fought their sons and sons their fathers in a terrible conflict that tore the land apart. Various parts of the country showed their support solidly in one way or the other—the West Country rallied for the King and though a poorer area, Wales too displayed similar, unflinching loyalty. (But in a practical sense, many of the principality's younger men joined up for want of good pay). By contrast, East Anglia and the Fenlands resolutely backed the Puritan side under Cromwell and were to prove important later regarding the formation of the New Model Army in 1645. There were, however, many places which displayed no particular sympathies to either faction, and some even wavered, their backing going from one side to the other.

Victims of Battle

Even several members of Oliver Cromwell's own family were Royalist supporters. Cromwell, a Huntingdon man, was well-educated and had been MP first for Huntingdon in 1628 and then for Cambridge in 1640. A supporter of Puritanism, he was first to show up as a brilliant soldier. Later, he would achieve the highest prominence as Lord Protector of the Realm.

Sir Edmund Verney, of Claydon House in Buckinghamshire, was not in sympathy with all the King's policies but chose to support the Crown nonetheless, in spite of his son's decision to back the Parliamentarians. No longer a young man, Sir Edmund was nevertheless proud to carry the Royal Standard at the disastrous Battle of Edgehill. Eventually struck down, he refused to yield the Standard and fell clasping it. In the ghastly brutality of battle, it was only after chopping off his hand that Cromwell's men could claim they had captured the precious flag.

Although his body was never recovered, Sir Edmund's hand, identified by a signet ring, was eventually placed in the crypt of Middle Claydon Church. Since then there have been numerous sightings of his troubled ghost, not only on the battlefield of Edgehill but also wandering around on the first floor of Claydon House, supposedly looking for his missing hand. With grim humour he is believed by some to still go knocking on the bedroom doors of guests at night!

Tactically, each side called for utmost discipline on the battlefield. It is amazing now to hear that opponents stood face-to-face, pikemen against pikemen (this was termed 'push of pike' when closely-packed companies drove at each other with 20ft. killing poles) and musketeers fired at point-blank range. Horrific injuries resulted and there was death in plenty. Indeed, during the Siege of York (1644) the Old Starr public-house was used as a primitive hospital for the wounded, and their screams are said to still echo from the cellars below, where severely damaged limbs were simply cut off while the patients were fully conscious, a bottle of whiskey offering little or no antidote.

Besides frequent battles, involving many thousands of men, there were many smaller skirmishes focused on individual castles, forts, manor-houses and hostelries. A legacy of hauntings recalls those dark days throughout the length and breadth of the country.

*   *   *

Corfe Castle in Dorset is a brooding ruin of a once great fortress, overlooking the village of the same name that lies far below. The Banks family, owners at the time of the Civil War were fervent Royalists and from 1643–45 it was Dame Mary Banks who oversaw defences when the castle was numerous times under siege by Cromwell's Parliamentarian troops. Their resolve held fast until someone betrayed the family, the result inevitably being that the place was blown up (or 'slighted') by Cromwell's forces. This was the unhappy fate of many fine castles and medieval halls during this period.

A weeping child has been heard in the area ever since, and a headless white lady drifts through the ruins. Some believe she is the spirit of the person who betrayed the Banks family, bringing them to financial ruin and the loss of their great castle. A phantom Roundhead soldier has also been seen by the staff of the National Trust that now owns the site.

One place lucky enough not to have been 'slighted' was Broughton Hall, just outside the market town of Eccleshall in Staffordshire. This black-and-white manor was once the seat of the Broughtons. Thomas Broughton was imprisoned by Cromwell at Stafford and fined, his wife forced to provide board and lodging for the Parliamentarian troops at Broughton. According to legend, the young heir of the estate leaned out of a window of the 2nd floor Long Gallery and taunted a group of soldiers by shouting 'I am the King!' On hearing this one of them fired, and the impulsive teenager fell back into the Gallery and managed to crawl into an adjoining room, where he died. One tale says he was wearing scarlet stockings at the time and these have been one of the distinctive features mentioned in various sightings of his ghost, earning him the nickname of 'Redsocks'. Another version suggests that it was his blood that stained his stockings red. It also seeped into the floor-timbers, the stains apparently still there as late as the 1920s, when the boards were renewed. The ghost of 'Redsocks' has often been seen in the Long Gallery and on the stairs. Broughton Hall is now owned by the Franciscan Order of St. Joseph. A nice touch, I think, is that the nuns still pray for the young man's spirit.

Mine Hosts to Ghosts

Many hostelries, besides harbouring ghosts from all ages, were very old even by the 17th century and were settings for brutal drama during the Civil War. Chequers of Doddington in Kent, for example, originated from the 12th century and even played 'mine host' to pilgrims on their way to Canterbury. It was here, too, that a Cavalier was murdered in an upstairs room and he can still be seen peering out of an overhanging window. Outside the Red Lion at Rusthall, which is also in Kent and dates from 1450, the clopping sound of a headless horseman wearing armour is often heard. The phantom is believed to be the ghost of one of Cromwell's men.

At Pulloxhill in Bedfordshire, the Cross Keys also hosts both the living and the dead, one of the latter being the phantom of another murdered Cavalier. The Royalist officer is quite often seen by guests about the place, recognisable by his pointed beard, plumed hat and cloak. An amorous Cavalier ghost even comes up behind the lady members of staff at the Tudor Rose, Fordingbridge in Hampshire, running his hands up and down their hips! Yet surely this cannot be the same ghost of a Royalist soldier who once came to the inn only to find his lady friend flirting with other men? As a result, *he* is said to have placed a curse on all women.

Probably the most celebrated phantom at the King's Head in Bird Street, Lichfield in Staffordshire, is that of a laughing cavalier. Challenged to a swordfight outside in the street by several of Cromwell's men, he courageously 'held his own' till being hacked to death. His remains were thrown into the cellar of the King's Head, where despite showing his wounds, his ghost appears with a laughing expression both in the hotel and walking the streets of Lichfield. Seemingly oblivious to the bustling traffic and even pedestrians, he simply passes through them.

As children, many people are much more psychically aware than later on in life, though some are able to retain and develop the gift. A small girl staying with her parents at the Highway Inn in Sourton, Devon a few years ago, claimed to have spoken to a man in green, who was wearing a large hat with a feather. This turned out to be the friendly phantom known as Samuel the Cavalier to the landlord and his guests. Appearing anywhere in the building, he has also been seen to pass through a wall where there was once a doorway leading to some old stables. He is believed to have been connected to the Battle of Sourton, the site of which is nearby.

*   *   *

Travelling to the North Wales coast along the Tarporley Road towards Chester, you will pass the Headless Woman Inn. It was once regarded as a joke against chatterboxes that 'only decapitation stopped their wagging tongues'. However, another explanation, as to the nature of the inn's name was offered on a notice-board in 1866, by the then landlord;

'A party of Cromwell's soldiers, engaged in hunting down the Royalists in the Chester district, visited Hockenhall Hall, but found that the family being warned of their coming had buried all the silver and other valuables and then fled for safety, leaving only a faithful old housekeeper in charge of the Hall, thinking it unlikely that the soldiers would do her any harm.

'The soldiers being incensed at finding nothing of value, locked up the housekeeper in a top room and proceeded to torture her to tell them where the valuables were hidden. She remained

faithful, and was finally murdered by the soldiers cutting off her head. Tradition says that afterwards, on numerous occasions, she was seen carrying her head under her arm, walking along the old bridle path between Hockenhall Hall and the spot where it comes out on the Tarporley Road near the public house.'

The 'faithful old housekeeper' was believed to be Grace Trigg, the cook. Alternatively, it is said that the soldiers actually hid her body—and the head—in the cottage at Duddon that later became the Inn.

*   *   *

Besides 'men of honour and believers in principle' on both sides during the Civil War, there was also the mercenary soldier, hired to fight. His motto was: 'I come not forth to do my country good, I come to rob and take my fill of pleasure'. There were also members of the dregs of society within the ranks, opportunists willing to rape and plunder. Small wonder at the many atrocities committed which found their place in the annals of the paranormal.

Another gruesome example was in 1648, following a Royalist defeat by Cromwell's men at Preston. At least 1,500 soldiers were taken to the parish church at Chapel-en-le-Frith,

Derbyshire where, for sixteen days, they were crammed into a very small space with hardly any room to move. Forty-four of them died in the horrendous crush. Many others were so weak they were left to die, while the survivors were taken away to an unknown fate.

Phantom King and Cavalier

With the prospects of both sides seeming fairly equal at the start of hostilities, things could have gone either way. So Cromwell made sure his troops became far better trained, particularly by 1645 and the decisive Battle of Naseby, with the formation of the New Model Army, founded by himself and Lord Fairfax. Only then did King Charles I and his cause begin to experience the tide of defeat which ultimately led to his capture, imprisonment, trial and execution in Whitehall, in January, 1649.

The king's headless body was taken for burial at Windsor, where his ghost is said to appear within the castle grounds. Some witnesses have even mentioned the likeness to that of the famous portrait by Van Dyck— though I do not know if his ghost appears physically complete or 'with his head tucked underneath his arm'.

In a twist to the usual tale at Athelhampton

Hall, Dorset, a pair of seemingly deadly opposed Cavalier duellists have been seen fiercely clashing swords in the Great Hall—but the drama ends not with the demise of one or the other, but with their sitting down at table for dinner together! Were they the ghosts of close friends eager to continue practising their swordplay in a later life? It is known that this Hall did have Royalist connections. Codnor Castle in Derbyshire, on the other hand, had no known dealings with the Civil War. Yet here there are claims that the phantom of an utterly dishevelled, exhausted Royalist soldier still appears among its ruins. At the Old Hall, Youlgreave in the White Peak District of Derbyshire, on a November night there can sometimes be glimpsed the phantom re-enactment of a duel 'to the death' between a Cavalier and Roundhead. They simply go on fighting *in perpetuum*.

*   *   *

It was on a hot, humid June afternoon in 1949 that a young couple were sitting near the site of the Battle of Naseby, their backs against a haystack. But in contrast to the former scene of devastation, the two were simply enjoying a picnic in the Leicestershire countryside. Suddenly, however, they became aware of a group of ghostly men, tired and dusty, pulling low, wooden carts in complete silence along a nearby ancient drovers road. Although far from dashing in appearance, with perspiration running down their faces, they could have been Cavaliers. The young lady described them as grimfaced, wearing black leather jerkins and boots, and thought that they might have been Parliamentarian soldiers. It was only later they were to learn that their visit to the area had coincided with the anniversary of the Battle of Naseby—14th June, 1645—in which the Royalists had been defeated.

Even by July the previous year, at the Battle of Marston Moor in North Yorkshire, the Royalists had lost at least 3,000 men, enhancing Cromwell's reputation as a strategist, while the King was seriously losing ground in the North. According to some, this battle is said to be re-fought at sunset on each date of its anniversary, although gunfire can be heard on other occasions. Many Royalist soldiers are buried in mass graves in the area and phantom soldiers have been seen by various people, including tourists, walking in ghostly formation in the dark along the A59. With their cloaks, wide-brimmed hats, cockades, high boots and shoulder-length hair, they have sometimes been mistaken for ordinary living people in fancy dress. Via cars lights, they have been identified by their tired and bedraggled appearance as remnants of the routed Royalists who at the blink of an eye, have simply disappeared. Just a small group—

possibly three or four—are these the ghosts of fallen soldiers, or survivors, still intent on escaping the wrath of Cromwell's pursuing Roundheads?

*   *   *

By 1651 and the Battle of Worcester, in which the young and future Charles II, with his army from Scotland was defeated, Cromwell had not only dealt with various factions within his own ranks but had also ruthlessly pacified Ireland and Scotland, convinced that he was 'executing the will of God'. Following the King's execution in 1649, both the Monarchy and the House of Lords were abolished. From 1653, after falling out with Parliament, Cromwell ruled as Lord Protectorate, even being offered the Crown in 1657, which he refused. Dying the following year he was succeeded by Richard, his son. Lacking the leadership qualities of his father, Richard Cromwell was unable to grapple with the ill-feeling that still festered between the Puritans and Royalists, resulting in an English Government close to anarchy. He resigned and a group—including George Monck, who had been Cromwell's Commander-in-Chief of Scotland—promoted the restoration of the Monarchy.

An invitation was sent to Charles in France, the young heir having offered himself as the legitimate candidate (and already had himself crowned Charles II in a ceremony at Scone after his father's execution) by his Declaration of Breda, a manifesto of moderation regarding religious and political tolerance Restored to his rightful throne Charles landed at Dover in May, 1660. Now Parliament would be heard and possess authority instead of the Crown.

Brooding and Bloody

This was not the end of things supernatural, however. Cromwell's house in Ely, Cambridgeshire is said to be haunted by a 'brooding male' presence, possibly Cromwell himself. The building is now used as the local tourist information centre and museum. His ghost is also said to haunt the Old Hall, in the village of Long Marston, North Yorkshire not far from the battlefield of that name, which he used as a base prior to the campaign.

In the year following the Restoration of 1660, there were those who saw fit to have Cromwell's body removed from Westminster Abbey for posthumous punishment. It was taken to the Red Lion Inn at Holborn, where it rested overnight. Put on a cart with the bodies of two of his closest allies Henry Ireton (d. 1651) and John Bradshaw (d. 1659) it was taken to Tyburn for ceremonial hanging and decapitation. Ever since the gruesome incident his ghost is said to haunt the Red Lion, and three cloaked figures—of Ireton, Bradshaw and Cromwell—are said to walk round Red Lion Square. Cromwell is also believed to haunt his alleged burial site at Connaught Place, the former Tyburn.

Cromwell's head was put on a pike at Westminster where it was either blown down by the elements or taken away in 1684 or 1688. Surprisingly, it was passed on to a series of keepers down the years, eventually being buried in a biscuit tin at Sidney Sussex Chapel in Cambridge as recently as March, 1960. He had been a student there during 1616–1617, and his ghost was witnessed as having returned several years after his head had found its final resting-place. Not only was the vision seen but several people complained about an obnoxious stench of rotting meat. A ghastly and ignominious end, in spite of the fact that he had been regarded as the 'Great Destroyer' of human life and much of England's architectural legacy at that time. For some his iconic image has joined those of St George and King Arthur, a leader ready to rise again in times of our country's greatest need.

Two further British examples of 'phantom aftermaths' of battle occurred a quarter of a century or more after the restoration of the monarchy when times were still unsettled. These were the battles of Sedgemoor and Killiecrankie.

On 6th July, 1685 the conflict at Sedgemoor in Somerset saw devastating defeat for James, Duke of Monmouth, the supposed illegitimate son of Charles II who had laid claim to the British Crown. His ghostly, bedraggled, peasant army has been seen many times since that date, attempting to escape the terrible carnage of that wet summer morning. His soldiers have also been witnessed in noisy as well as silent combat with those of James II, his uncle. The spectre of the Duke himself is said to appear annually, riding on horseback as he repeats his successful escape from the battlefield through the morning fog. He was captured by the Sussex militia a few days later and executed on 15th July on Tower Hill.

Viscount John Graham of Claverhouse, best known as Bonnie Dundee, had waited all day with his 2,500 Jacobite Highlanders near the Pass of Killiecrankie. There was a sense of doom for earlier, having seen a spectral bloodstained head he had taken it as an omen of his own impending death. The date was 27th July, 1689, the troops of William III were arriving for military engagement and as the evening sun flooded the valley, the Highlanders suddenly charged downhill in full might. Within minutes the 3,500 British troops were completely routed, taken aback by the tartan savagery and blood-curdling war-cries. Yet as they fled, a single shot rang out killing Bonnie Dundee, the omen of doom proving true. And on the evening of 27th July, it is said that the strongly psychic area is covered by a ghostly glow—perhaps the lingering of the blood-red sunset that bathed the valley on that fateful date in 1689.

4
PHANTOM BLACK DOGS—
AND A PRINCE'S SCOTTISH ARMY

' . . . in shape o' beast
A towsy tyke, black, grim and large'

Tam O' Shanter
Robert Burns

Real dogs, dead dogs, ghost dogs or dogs that have never existed at all—or have they? We now enter the highly-charged stuff and dreams of profound legend—the world of the alien spectral hound or ghostly Black Shuck, fierce guardian of many a dark road, bridle way or path where death has occurred whether by accident or intent. This has little to do with the spirit of a well-loved and departed pet, but is something of a far more dubious reputation, especially in its connections with the aftermath of bloody skirmish and war.

Usually perceived as about the size of a calf, Black Shuck has been described as having a black shaggy coat (either bristly or smooth), blazing eyes the size of saucers and teeth sometimes running with blood. Some of these phantom hounds can even be grey, white or yellow while others, known as 'shape-shifters', are able to alter their size and shape into human form or even represent other animals. In many mythologies we find that the gods were able to transform themselves into any shape, including those of animals (including Black Dogs) and birds. Many spectral dogs, it is sometimes believed, are the spirits of wicked people. During the 19th century, when suicide was considered a crime, it is said that a man who hanged himself near Shrewsbury returned in the form of a Black Dog.

But despite the legend and mythology, what are the real origins of this beast?

While I was working on my book *Living with Ghosts*, a dowser called Stephen Wilde told me that he believed that Black Dogs were actually thought forms that were marshalled into existence by Celtic tribal holy men or Druids. Former occupants of these islands, they had a considerable knowledge of medicines and, he was convinced, a capacity for the occult that included the bringing into being of thought forms (or tulpas). 'My belief,' he added, 'is that these dogs were simply protective devices, to roam and protect burial sites and sacred places.'

Another source of the Black Dog phenomenon could well have been its association with the jackal-headed god Anubis of Ancient Egypt, some 3,000 years ago. Deeply respected as a guide for the dead, he would see them safely through the Underworld. In Pre-classical Greece it was

Cerebus, a three-headed dog, who acted as a guardian over the dead. Black Dogs could also have had their origins in Ancient Greece, where it was believed that Diana, the Goddess of Hunting, rode one of them across a moonlit sky at night. The Romans later blended these myths with their own and so it was that Caesar's legions brought the beliefs to Britain.

According to early Anglo Saxon chronicles, both Anubus and Cerebus were considered as passive guardians concerned mainly with passage of that hinterland between the quick and the dead. Yet during the late Anglo Saxon period the role of these beasts began to change, becoming symbolic of death and destruction throughout the land.

*   *   *

The old *Annals of St Bertin* reported that for four hundred years or so, from the 6th to 10th centuries AD, many Christian establishments throughout Northern Europe were ruthlessly attacked by the fierce heathen Viking hordes—basic history most of us were taught at school. One entry describes such attacks having taken place in Gaul in 846 AD and in parts of Aquitaine where wolves gathered in groups of 300 strong to form formidable battle lines, charging mercilessly to the detriment of anything or anyone in their way.

This actually smacks of Viking strategy, as

the more passive forms of Black Dog previously represented by Anubis and Cerebus were replaced by the Viking belief in the Nordic god Odin, God of Victory, father of the slain and ruler of an army of warrior spirits. In old English the Vikings were indeed described as 'wolves of slaughter', particularly after the Battle of Maldon in 991 AD, and in fact some of the fiercest Danish fighters actually wore wolf pelts. Others used large, fierce 'war dogs' brought in from Scandinavia, whose slavering violence added further distress and horror to the victims. The Christian Anglo Saxon population living here in the British Isles referred to such beasts as Scucca (Shuck), alias the Devil, and it is possible that such terrible images may still run deep within the human psyche, despite the actual living memory having long gone.

In Ghostly Packs

Most parts of Britain have borne witness to these Black Hounds of Hell in varying forms. Trash, the Ghost Dog of Formby waterfront has been spotted on numerous occasions and is also known as 'The Skriker' due to its rasping cries. These are supposed to foretell death or serious misfortune to anyone unlucky enough to hear them. Described as a gigantic black hound with large, luminous eyes, the beast prowls by night along the shore between Formby and Ainsdale but leaves no footprints in the sand. Legend tells of a drunken man who, on encountering it one night, was so terrified that he struck it with his stick—which passed straight through the spectral beast!

But there can be another side to these legendary animals. In his book *Ghosts of Derbyshire* Clarence Daniel writes about the time his mother, then a young girl, felt frightened as she was walking home one dark night along a deserted stretch of road towards Calver. Suddenly her fears dissolved as she discovered a huge white dog, which she sensed to be friendly and protective, walking at her side. When they reached her village with its lights and busier road, the beast left her and to her amazement walked straight through a solid stone wall.

In the desolate Fenlands of East Anglia a spectral animal has been seen with a single eye in the centre of its head blazing yellow or scarlet. The coast near to Cromer is another of its haunts and it trots along lonely lanes at night near the Norfolk Broads at Neatishead and Wicken Fen, near Newmarket. In Suffolk there are tales of Black Shuck (or Scarfe, or Galleytrot, as it is known in those parts), a fierce, ghostly dog that roams the marshes.

The spectre is known by various names in other parts of the country. For example,

Shriker or Hooter in Lancashire; Baghest, Guytrash or Padfoot in Yorkshire; Boggie or Dobby in the Lake District; Cappel in Westmorland; Muckle Black Tyke in Scotland; Gwillgi in Wales; Moddey Dhoo in the Isle of Man. Various other names connected with the Spectral Hound include those of Hellbeast, Shug Monkey, Old Snarlyon and Gabriel's Rachehounds. In Europe it is known as Hell Hound and in Africa it is often referred to as Wolhaarhond. One type, known as Barghest supposedly brings death to all who see it. It has been described as being large, black and shaggy, with eyes as large as saucers. Endowed with supernatural powers, it is found in churchyards, having been reported in various places both in Britain and France.

In Wales, Gwyllgi or supernatural dogs of Darkness have also been similarly witnessed but with glowing red eyes. However the appearance of Cwn Cyrff (corpse dogs), Cwn Wybr (sky dogs) or Cwn Annwn (dogs of the underworld) are said to vary from the more popular concept of phantom hounds, being small, greyish red, sometimes speckled and led by a black-horned figure.

To actually witness a pack of any of these also means death to the beholder, though they are more often heard than seen, with their eerie barking and blood-curdling howls. A pack rushing airborne in hot pursuit of their prey—souls condemned to eternal torture—

they have been described as being 'black, with fiery eyes and teeth sprinkled all over with blood'. If the pack is seen hovering above some chosen property this usually means ill-fortune or even death to the unfortunate soul or souls within. Particularly in dangerous occupations like quarrying or mining, people have always superstitiously tended to regard them as portents of disaster.

By contrast (though it is difficult to see how) others have described the sound made by the pack as representing 'the music of angels transporting some blessed soul to its eternal home.' More scientifically, it has been suggested that their ghostly wailings could be attributed to the calls of the bean goose during its migratory flight. Nonetheless, the West Country is said to have a pack of phantom wild Black Dogs whose ghastly howls have been heard right across the vast, desolate area of Dartmoor.

*   *   *

Such a pack need not be in pursuit of human souls, however. On All Hallows Eve the spectral hunter Gabriel Ratchets, with his hounds, is still said to ritualistically pursue a milk-white doe from Cliviger Gorge through Eagle's Crag in the Vale of Todmorden, in West Yorkshire. In Leeds, such hounds referred to as Gabble Ratchets (in Derbyshire, also known as Rache-hounds) are believed to be the souls of dead, un-baptized small children who, unable to enter Paradise, return to haunt their hapless parents.

Phantom Black Dogs may be seen where murder has been committed and (so it is said) where a suicide was buried at the crossroads, so that his or her soul would be unable to find which way to go. Many such places have retained feelings of negative black energy, so much so that neither animals nor human beings will stay there any longer than they need. Two such places, according to Doug Pickford in his *Earth Mysteries of the Three Shires* can be found in Cheshire—at the Standing Stone in Macclesfield Forest and at Windmill Wood, Alderley Edge. This tradition still lingers on despite our more enlightened approach to suicide nowadays.

In Scotland the phantom dogs are said to be green, the size of a small cow and they are shortish tailed. Also known as faery dogs, they bark three times and anyone who listens is wise to make 'haste away' before hearing the third bark, otherwise they are said to be doomed.

Doom and Defeat

In England, Black Shuck haunts old roads and

as we have seen, is especially active in places of high tension and trauma. It is believed the creatures could well draw their energy from ley-lines, particularly where an old road is actually built on such a line. They also act as guardians along routes taken by armies and are believed to be connected with the retreat of Bonnie Prince Charlie and his Scottish Army in December, 1745 across the wild Staffordshire Moorlands and the Peak District of Derbyshire. It is only with hindsight that we can see by how narrow a margin the cause was lost, and how close the Prince and his forces came to succeeding in their mission to unseat King George II and send him and his Hanoverian court back to Germany.

At the time, opponents to the Jacobite Cause were busy trying to spread alarm and panic throughout the country by various means. One of the stories from this period concerns The Angel, an old inn at Kendal in the Lake District, which was known to be haunted by some unknown ghost. When the town was occupied by the Scottish Army as it passed through on its way south, the landlord and his wife, together with their children, hurriedly left the building to find a safe refuge. In the confusion they discovered that their youngest child had been left behind, but consoled themselves with the thought that not even Highlanders would harm a baby. Back at the Angel, so the story goes, the infant was sleeping, blissfully unaware of what might happen, when a group of soldiers discovered it. One of them moved, reaching out his hand towards the child when suddenly, the ghostly figure that haunted the building appeared. The terrified soldiers left immediately, leaving the child secure and unharmed in safe (phantom?) hands.

After disembarking from a French vessel at Moidart in Scotland a few weeks before, the Prince and his Scottish Army had advanced into England via Carlisle, having routed the English redcoats at Prestonpans. Supporters rallied to the Jacobite Cause, but the Prince, who had been promised full support from the Welsh Jacobites for some time, found that now they were needed, there was silence. One who did join Bonnie Prince Charlie was David Morgan of Penycraig near Merthyr, by profession a barrister in London. He rode north together with Richard and William Vaughan of Courtfield, members of a Monmouthshire Roman Catholic family. Morgan quickly gained the trust of the Prince, becoming his counsellor. He was even permitted to ride at Charles' side.

When they had come as far south as Derby, the Prince held vital discussions with his officers at Exeter House to thrash out the burning question of whether they should continue south. They were dependant on hearsay support from Jacobites farther down the route (which might not materialise) and risked further likely encounters with the unknown strength of English redcoat soldiers. A vote was taken and Bonnie Prince Charlie—who would have continued—was beaten by one vote. Interestingly, though Exeter House was demolished in 1854, the panelling from the drawing room was saved, and reinstated in Derby Museum. Some visitors say they have 'picked up' a feeling of dire depression and foreboding in the reconstructed drawing room and this sense of doom may well have been retained by the panelling—the heartfelt despair of a seemingly hapless prince.

He had cause to feel such despair, for a week after erring on the side of caution and retreating from Derby, the Scottish Army placed a terrible price tag on its head. Ironically, not two days into the retreat, a messenger arrived to say that the Welsh Jacobites were ready to join the Prince's Cause. Too late! The demoralised army was already breaking up, some Highland soldiers being killed long before they reached the Scottish border. Others, afraid and disillusioned, 'disappeared' from the ranks and found shelter in the surrounding countryside, gaining employment on isolated farms and smallholdings along the way—many eventually even marrying into their adopted communities. The majority, however—some 5,000 exhausted men, greatly outnumbered—

faced the infamous Duke of Cumberland and his 9,000 English redcoat soldiers on Culloden Moor in April the following year. This was the last pitched battle to be fought on British soil, finishing in just over one hour.

There were few survivors. The Highlanders, or Jacobites were slaughtered in their thousands, the English soldiers afterwards massacring all the wounded they could find lying on the battlefield. Those suffering from lesser wounds were ruthlessly pursued in their attempts to escape and hacked down. All this was done at the order of the Duke of Cumberland, a course of action which earned him his nickname of 'Butcher'. The English losses were around fifty.

David Morgan had earlier decided against withdrawing to Scotland with Bonnie Prince Charlie, telling him he would sooner hang than starve. Captured at Stone in Staffordshire, he was eventually sentenced to be hanged, drawn and quartered. His ghost has apparently never been seen, surprising when considering that such a ghastly method of punishment was implemented at such a comparatively late period. The 18th century has often been referred to as the Age of Enlightenment, when logic and reason were to the fore, yet on the other hand, it was obviously still an age of great cruelty and violence. (It was actually in 1817, after their murder trial at the Shire Hall, Derby, that the Pentrich Martyrs were the last people in Britain sentenced to be hung, drawn and quartered.)

Richard and William Vaughan both survived Culloden, having fought gallantly, before finally escaping to Spain. Bonnie Prince Charlie also managed to narrowly escape from Scotland by ship and went back to France, never to return.

A cairn and mound now occupy the tragic battle site of Culloden which, psychically, still emanates a terrible sadness. From time to time, especially at dusk, dead and injured Highlanders are still seen staggering around dazedly on the battlefield. Some phantom soldiers in tartan have been seen still in combat with English Redcoats while battle cries, clashes of swords, musket-fire and all the terrified sounds of men dying have also been heard. On one occasion a visitor saw the body of a dark-haired, handsome young Highlander lying on the top of the mound and when she approached him, she noticed his dirty, muddy clothes and the old-fashioned cut of the material. His face looked unnaturally pale, and suddenly realising what she was really looking at—a dead phantom soldier—she left the site *post haste*.

*　　　*　　　*

On one of the small, wooded islands on Loch Morar near to Mallaig, the ghostly figure of

Simon Fraser, Lord Lovat, has been seen. This was his 'bolt-hole' after Culloden, where Cumberland's soldiers eventually rounded him up. Mr J.W. Whyle of Glasgow wrote to author and ghost hunter Peter Underwood, reporting that he had actually seen Lord Lovat still there—'A very heavy old chap, with a fat florid face and suffering badly from gout!'

Scottish soldiers of the same period were also witnessed in the Cuillin Hills on the Isle of Skye, during the 1950s. Whether or not they were connected with the '45 one cannot say.

A song written in the romantic tradition and performed by the music-hall star-of-old Sir Harry Lauder, had its origins in the '45 Jacobite Rebellion. Of two Highland prisoners of the English redcoats, one is about to be released while the other is due to be shot. Reference by the latter to *'Oh, ye'll tak the High Road, and I'll tak the Low Road /And I'll be in Scotland before ye'* means that his comrade has got to make the journey home—presumably—on foot, but he who faces execution will be back there, via the Low Road (the spiritual route) before him. And sadly he says of himself: *'For me and my true love will never meet again/On the bonnie, bonnie banks of Loch Lomond.'*

As the Scottish Army had come a few months before, so it retreated back in December 1745 through the Derbyshire Peaks and the high Moorlands of Staffordshire—arguably a part of the British Isles most richly endowed with folklore and paranormal mystique—leaving its spectral footprints across the landscape and embedded even deeper into the realms of legend.

Gun Hill has a commanding view over the Staffordshire Moorlands, and is part of the Old Route south of Manchester and down into the market town of Leek that the Prince and his men took in those fateful December days. Here you can almost slice the powerfully weird atmosphere all the year round, and are uncomfortably aware of watchful eyes of the many unseen. My wife Dilys and I visited the area on a bright, though windy spring afternoon and Dilys in particular found the place near the top where we parked the car, quite dire and threatening. It was in this vicinity, we discovered later, that criminals were once hanged.

Many ghostly tales have evolved around the failed attempt by Bonnie Prince Charlie to wrest the English Crown from the House of Hanover and restore it back to the Stuarts. This was failure—but what a glorious failure.

81

Inevitably with examples of this kind, we can speculate endlessly on thoughts of 'what might have happened, if only . . . '

On his advance south what did this fascinating man, then in his mid-twenties, look like? Seeing him enter the market town of Leek in Staffordshire, a Mr Joshua Toft of Haregate Hall wrote memorably:

> '*Bonnie Prince Charlie . . . I saw him march at the head of a regiment on foot. They say he has mostly done so since he left Edinburgh. He appears to be about five feet ten inches high, of a comely aspect, dressed after the Highland fashion, his face somewhat marked with smallpox, and I think reddish-haired. He had on a light wig, a broad blue ribbon over one shoulder and on the other his plaid of light green.*'

*   *   *

To this day many ghosts of Jacobite soldiers defiantly haunt the Old Route right back up to Scotland itself, while phantom Black Dogs attend their graves. At the village of Swinscoe (situated along the Leek–Ashbourne Road) three Jacobite soldiers were ambushed and another ghostly Black Dog guards their graves.

After appearing at a charity concert in Ashbourne in 1962 the actress Diana Dors stayed at a cottage in Swinscoe and on waking up during the night, she saw a man with long, flowing hair standing in her bedroom. Initially angry because she thought it was a fan intruding on her privacy, she realised it was the spectre of someone from another age, looking exhausted and dishevelled. Subsequent enquiries indicated she had actually encountered a phantom Jacobite soldier, probably one of those killed in Swinscoe during the retreat.

*   *   *

While the Scottish Army (of about 7,000 men) was still in and around Derby, a group of some 70 were sent on to secure Swarkstone Bridge, several miles south of the county town, which was the only way over the River Trent between Nottingham and Burton. When the decision was taken to abandon the march down to London they were recalled for the journey back up North—but a retreating army is always vulnerable to attack and that of Bonnie Prince Charlie was no exception. Ever since, many people around Swarkstone have reported hearing sounds of clashing swords and the thud and clatter of the horses' hooves of an invisible cavalry, becoming louder as they approach before fading within a few minutes.

Oxhay Farm ('The Red Lion Inn', back in 1745) in the village of Bradnop, near to Leek, was where two Jacobite soldiers quarrelled after an evening's drinking and one killed the other. The victim was buried behind the farm, where a Black Shuck now haunts the road outside. Legend has it that phantom hounds are also connected with one or two local wells and some people are not surprised that the area has its fair share of Black Dogs. They believe the area around Bradnop contains many secrets of Earth Magic and Mystery. The same could be said of the village of Ipstones, a few miles away, a place where all the wells are said to be guarded by spirits. Years ago, prior to mains water being supplied, residents only went for water during daylight hours and even then with caution. One well in particular was guarded by a large, spectral Black Dog and there are stories reporting how whenever someone has dared to strike the beast with a stick, the latter simply passed through its form and the Dog then disappeared.

Curse of a Ghostly Drum

> *'Yet portion of that unknown land*
> *Will Hodge forever be;*
> *His homely Northern breast and brain*
> *Grow to some Southern tree,*
> *And strange-eyed constellation reign*
> *His stars eternally.'*
>
> *Drummer Hodge*
> Thomas Hardy

It was at Endon—four miles south-west of Leek—and possibly a place with a good deal less of the Earth Magic, that some of the Scottish soldiers on their way south were billeted at the home of one Squire Murhall. Seething with quiet resentment, he nevertheless had to put up with the unwelcome company, who helped themselves to much of his food and drink, warming themselves against the cold December weather around his fireside. Once they had departed for Leek, the Squire and a small band of helpers gave chase at some distance, and managed to snatch just one straggling member of the Scottish Army—a fifteen-year-old drummer-boy called Tam. Terribly, so the story goes, they brought their struggling captive back and proceeded to skin him alive!

Squire Murhall then had the boy's skin stretched and made into a drum, which according to one of two legends about it, was hung in the local church of St. Luke's. Many heads of cattle died and crop failures occurred as a result of this obscene and dastardly act, until the drum was finally taken away and buried. The other, a more likely tale, was that on hearing of Tam's terrible death—and yes, news could travel fast even in those times—a handful of his comrades returned and exacted savage punishment on Squire Murhall, who was left crippled for the rest of his life. Both legends, however, agree that the ghost of young Tam has been seen regularly ever since that dreadful day in 1745 in an area of fields and woods between Endon and Leek, which have a strange and brooding atmosphere.

Is this a locality which retains feelings of negative black energy after the dreadful deed once done there? Although Tam's brutal murder might still have its reverberations, perhaps like Bradnop this is another area of potential Earth Magic—particularly since a very ancient burial mound that still feels very powerful is situated close by. The power is such that according to dowser Stephen Wilde: 'Legend has it that lions have been seen within the area of the mound—though it is more likely to be the shaggy, large-eyed giant dog, or 'shuck'.

5

SHADES OF THE AMERICAN CIVIL WAR

*'As I sat musing, 'twas a host in dark
array,
With their horses and their cannon
wheeling onward to the fray,
Moving like a shadow to the fate the
brave must dree,
And behind me roared the drums, rang
the trumpets of the sea.'*

The Song of Soldiers
Walter de la Mare

To this day, the phantom of a tall, gaunt-looking man is said to walk the streets of Harpers Ferry, Virginia, USA bearing an exact likeness to the militant protestor John Brown, whose avowed intent was to destroy the 'peculiar institution' of slavery, which he regarded as a sin against God. Asked by tourists to pose with them for photographs the gentleman willingly obliges, but when developed they reveal nothing but a gap where he had stood.

Originally arriving in town on 16th October 1859 with 21 followers, John Brown had already had five pro-slavery supporters killed by the sword at Pottawatomie Creek in

Kansas. In Virginia (one of the states that would later break away from the Union) he called for rebellion at Harpers Ferry, armed with weapons secretly supplied by New England abolitionists as well as having captured the local government armoury. His aim was to march south with an army of freed slaves, but this was immediately dashed by the arrival of a company of US Marines led by Colonel Robert E. Lee. Several people were killed in the skirmish and Brown was accused of treason and subsequently hanged in Charles Town, Virginia—a hero in the eyes of Northerners, a dire threat in the opinion of the South. Despite his death Brown had lit the fuse that was to ignite the American Civil War two years later.

The industrial Northern states had both prospered and expanded, taking in many immigrants, mainly from Europe, who subscribed to that prosperity. Their crops consisted of wheat, rye and many others that provided staple food. Although slavery had been accepted in what was to become the United States since 1619, the Northern states with their Quaker and Puritan origins soon rejected the system, abhorring the idea of human slavery that burgeoned in the Southern states. The latter, more sparsely populated and less prosperous despite individual families growing rich on their large plantations, had only tobacco and cotton as their main crops and both were labour intensive. Many Southerners felt superior to both the immigrants in the North and to their own black slaves, in spite of the fact that their economy was dependant mainly on slave labour.

*   *   *

The Southern states also believed strongly in their own rights, no longer feeling answerable to the Union which was powerfully upheld in the North. 1860 saw Abraham Lincoln elected as President, a staunch upholder too of the Union and a critic of slavery. This was too much for the Southern states, who defied the Constitution by leaving the Union to form their own Confederacy, and voting in their own president, Jefferson Davies. Many officers and soldiers of Southern origin resigned from the Union to join the Confederate Army, ready for the inevitable fight. One of the Union strategies would be to block the Southern ports in an attempt to cut both supplies of food and vital equipment for their war effort, and to cripple the Confederacy's economy.

Conflict started with a series of relative small skirmishes but after the first year (1861) it was to develop into one of the bloodiest of wars ever to have been fought in the country. Over 600,000 people were to die, not only on the battlefield but through disease and exposure to atrocious weather conditions; the vengeance and cruelty of war that often prevailed gave substance to dire and long-lasting, paranormal occurrences.

Bloody Battles

On April 10–11th 1862, Fort Pulaski on Tybee Island in the mouth of the Savannah River was heavily bombarded from neighbouring Cockspur Island by eleven Unionist batteries. The Confederates surrendered. The fort was then used to hold over 500 Confederate prisoners, who by the winter of 1864–5 were being detained in terrible conditions; there was no heat and they were starved in retaliation for similar treatment being forced on Unionist prisoners elsewhere. Because of the death and suffering that occurred in this place, visitors to Fort Pulaski have encountered many ghosts including phantom soldiers from the Civil War still patrolling the ramparts by moonlight.

Also in April 1862 during the two-day battle at Shiloh on the Tennessee River, the Confederates under General Albert S. Johnson gained the upper hand by launching a surprise attack on the Unionists, who were led by General Ulysses S. Grant. Fierce fighting ensued, the Confederates gaining ground. By the end of the second day Unionist forces had crossed the river, concentrating their artillery on the Southern forces with gunboats also firing on their positions. Johnson was mortally wounded and the Confederates fell back with 10,700 dead and wounded. The Northerners in their turn had only just avoided defeat, with 13,000 of their own men killed or wounded.

After General Johnson's death command passed to his second, General Pierre G.T. Beauregard, one of Alabama's senior generals. Considered one of the best, he had seen the first shots of the war fired at Fort Sumter in Charleston Harbour the previous year. Returning eventually to his home town, New Orleans the General might well be considered to have taken some of his dead back with him. His house, Number 113 Charles Street, is said to be occupied by many spectral Confederate soldiers who roam its rooms and corridors. Even scenes depicting Shiloh—men bayoneting each other, the ground littered with corpses, the injured crying out in pain, all accompanied by the sounds of loud gunfire—are said to re-enact themselves within the house as though thrown onto a large screen. The tired, broken figure of General Beauregard himself is said to appear whispering sadly the fateful words: 'Shiloh! Shiloh!'

*   *   *

September 17th 1862 was marked as the dawn when the most blood was spilt in a single day of the war—at Antietam in Maryland. Of the 23,000 killed, injured or missing, 540 men had belonged to the thousand-strong Irish Brigade from New York. Flying their green banner embellished with the Celtic harp, shouting 'Faugh a ballagh! Faugh a ballagh!' ('Clear the way!) they threw themselves against the savagery of Confederate gunfire. Their action helped to clear a way through, actually forcing the Confederates, under the command of Robert E. Lee, to retreat across the Potomac River into Virginia from where they had come. At Antietam, now a National Historic Site, the rangers there believe those gallant Irishmen could still be around since strange chanting sounds have been heard besides the usual ones associated with a phantom battle. Are they still advancing with determined cries of 'Faugh a ballagh!', perhaps?

During the Battle of Fredericksburg on unlucky 13th December 1862 the Unionist General Ambrose Burnside gave orders for ill-conceived uphill attacks on the Confederate forces, which resulted in 12,000 losses compared to half that number of Confederate deaths. Amid the mayhem, Sergeant Richard Kirkland repeatedly filled water canteens for his dying Union comrades. His ghost haunts the former battlefield, still tending the wounded, whose agonised moans are clearly audible.

At the Cashtown Inn in Cashtown, eight miles west of Gettysbourg, the Confederate Generals Robert E. Lee and A.P. Hill conferred on 1st July, 1863. The inn, which served as Hill's headquarters, is haunted by a phantom Confederate soldier whose footsteps in the attic are clearly heard. Also, for some reason, he tends to knock on the door of Room 4 after dark. For an assignation with a woman long gone?

Riding in Ghostly Ranks

Official reports present only facts known at the time and it is only afterwards that these can be challenged as only partly true or even not accurate at all. Researching the Battle of Gettysburg I found two slightly different versions of what happened at one particular spot—Little Round Top. The first outlined the known historical facts of the tragic event—the other, while no doubt just as true to those present at the time, also takes into account the heightened state of awareness of the moment, where the contagion of fear seems to have suddenly manifested itself as a vision of divine intervention.

History states (rightly) that some ten months after Antietam Robert E. Lee, with his Confederate forces, was again moving north from the Shenandoah Valley into Pennsylvania. Confronted by Union forces outside the small town of Gettysburg, three days of fierce and bitter fighting ensued. By the second day (2nd July, 1863) the Confederates had occupied the town while the Unionists with 90,000 men had secured Cemetery Ridge and Cemetery Hill, Calps Hill and Little Round Top to the south. Due to a strategic blunder, however, they left themselves exposed on their left flank and a Confederate division headed for Little Round Top, managing to occupy the lower slopes but failing to make it to the top through the savage resistance offered by the Unionists.

It is also said that after two hours those Unionists—the 20th Maine—were actually running short of ammunition. With the Confederate approach a desperate cry went up for more ammunition and suddenly a ghostly figure appeared with blazing sword held aloft, mounted on a brilliant white stallion. With a tricorn on his head, dressed in a uniform of the American Revolution, the dazed men recognised none other than George Washington himself, dead for more than sixty-five years, who had returned to lead them to victory.

'Fix bayonets!' the cry rang out. Then:

'Charge!'

Thus inspired, the men from Maine charged swiftly downhill catching the Confederates by surprise. They quickly gave way: and another day of fierce fighting followed, leaving Robert E. Lee with no alternative but to retreat, never again to invade the northern states.

Residents in and around Gettysburg vouch that on particularly warm summer nights, a noble figure on a brilliant white stallion—both enveloped in a luminous mist—moves across the battlefield, sparks flying wherever the hooves of the faithful steed strike the ground. People who live along what is now Route 116 also experience the awfulness of that doomed retreat on the nights of 4th and 5th July, when the sight of a long procession of phantom wagons can be seen to pass by, escorted by equally phantom Confederate cavalrymen in their grey uniforms. The desperate cries of hundreds of phantom injured on board may still be heard. As part of Lee's retreating army, the actual convoy of wagons bearing casualties is believed to have stretched for more than 17 miles.

*　　　*　　　*

During restoration of Fort McAllister State Park some years ago, workers refused to stay overnight because of reported happenings which unnerved them. Still retained on the ether were strange, eerie echoes, a kind of pulsing nocturnal 'heartbeat' attributed to the ghosts still present of Union and Confederate soldiers who had died there. In December 1864, having left Atlanta in flames, Unionist General William T. Sherman with two large columns of troops crossed Georgia leaving a wide belt of destruction in their wake. Nearing Savannah, it was Fort McAllister that provided the last Confederate stronghold in the area and after only token resistance, the garrison was quickly taken. This resulted in Confederate General William Hardee and 10,000 men abandoning Savannah and retreating quickly north into South Carolina. The fall of Fort McAllister marked the end of conflict in Georgia.

Any soldier in the American Civil War—even if only slightly injured—still ran considerable risk of death through infection through lack of hygiene, particularly in field hospitals. If taken prisoner, as we have already gathered, the odds of coming out alive were weighed heavily against for both sides were equally guilty of cruelly mistreating prisoners. At Andersonville, which was considered by both sides to be Georgia's hell-hole, 33,000 Unionist prisoners were detained in wretchedness and squalor in a miserable 27 acres, mostly under canvas. Sickness and depression caused men to wander around vacantly or lie about comatose for long periods, some simply giving up. The prison at Andersonville was opened in 1864 and over 13,000 men died there. Starvation was common, rations being two ounces of rotting pork plus a little bread and rice—for as the war progressed, the Confederacy could hardly afford to feed its own soldiers, let alone captured Unionists.

By way of expediency, it was the camp commandant Captain Henry Wirz who was the only officer found guilty of war crimes in November, 1865 and hanged, in spite of the fact that he had tried to obtain better conditions in the camp. In his pathetic wrath he has been seen wandering through the camp and lingering at the graves in the cemetery. With conditions so extreme and desperate, prisoners had even robbed fellow prisoners, sometimes even killed them—six of the worst offenders eventually being hanged. The anniversary of their deaths (11th July) sees their spectres return 'with eyes popping out', their necks looped with stinking, rotten rope. There seem remarkably few hauntings here in view of the huge death toll but there could well prevail a general miasma and atmosphere of wretched negativity that might take centuries to wear off.

Griffon House on Constance Street in New Orleans was another place used not only as a barracks, but also as a prison. It, too, has retained vivid, 'living' memories of the Civil

War. When the advancing Unionists occupied the city, strict orders dictated that anyone caught looting would be shot, and two of their own soldiers were detained and locked up in Griffon House. On discovering they were actually Confederate spies posing as Union soldiers they were immediately condemned to death, but rather than face hanging or being shot by the military, they bribed their guard for his pistols and shot each other simultaneously through the heart. Subsequent occupiers of Griffon House have vividly experienced the sound of marching feet and men singing 'John Brown's Body'. One woman saw blood dripping through the ceiling yet on rushing upstairs, she found nothing.

Sad Deaths are Mourned

One of the great tragedies of this Civil War was that many generals, including Confederate Robert E. Lee and even more officers who faced each other across the battle lines, had graduated from the same US Military Academy at West Point. As a cadet in 1860, George Armstrong Custer from Ohio helped to celebrate the graduation of his great friend Stephen Ramseur, a fellow cadet three years his senior. Ironically, by October 1864 Custer, then a cavalry brigadier with the Union Army, was on a trail of destruction in the Shenandoah Valley while conversely Ramseur, at 27 a Confederate major general and his men were determined to stop him. Emotionally however, both were soon to be sadly reconciled.

Leading his division, having had two horses shot from under him, Ramseur was mounting a third when he was blasted in the chest. Suddenly demoralised, his division gave up the struggle and Ramseur was captured. At Union headquarters in Belle Grove Mansion in nearby Middletown, he was found to be mortally wounded. At his bedside were gathered his former comrades from West Point—a grieving Custer, Henry du Pont, artillery captain, and a cavalry general, Wesley Merritt.

Through some kind of time-slip over a century later, a visitor to Belle Grove entered this room. Unaware of what had happened there, he saw a man in Confederate grey lying on a bed, surrounded by several others in blue uniforms. Thinking he was intruding, he mumbled 'Sorry!' and hurried out, assuming they had been actors rehearsing, although he had picked up an overpowering sense of futility and sadness. Later, looking through a book, he recognised pictures of Ramseur and Custer, the latter being one of the men in blue he had seen at the bedside.

October 19th in the same year saw a

surprise dawn attack by the Confederates, under General Jubal A. Early, on the Unionists at Cedar Creek in Virginia. Routing the VIII and XIX corps, they assumed victory was theirs. The Union commander, Major General Philip Sheridan, however, arriving from Winchester at that crucial moment, quickly rallied his shaken troops and launched a savage counter-attack on the Confederate Army (of 21,000 men at the start). This time it proved a true catastrophe for the Southern cause. In deep, brooding remembrance, Cedar Creek still notes the tremendous loss of life on both sides. Small wonder it is widely accepted as 'one of the most haunted battlefields of the American Civil War', with its phantom musket-fire sometimes heard by tourists—previously unaware of the facts—canons, eerie bugle calls and cries from the dying and severely wounded.

During 1864, as the war swept on, Ulysses S. Grant, the Union's Commander-in-Chief, slowly pressurised the Southern cause into eventual submission, despite huge casualties taken by his own forces. Throughout the latter part of the war Union raiding parties laid to waste wide swathes of Alabama, ruining the Southern economy so that it would take years to recover.

By March 1865, the whole of the Shenandoah Valley had been taken for the Union, with General Robert E. Lee having been trapped for months around Petersburg, Virginia. Trying to break out to join fellow Confederates to the south, his Army was blocked. And so Fort Stedman, part of the Unionist battle line, was attacked, the Confederate advance failing miserably and sacrificing at least 5,000 men, some of whose unquiet spirits are still around. Visitors to the area have also reported seeing phantom Union soldiers on the hills, waiting to do battle where a Confederate counter-attack had gone wrong. Chillingly there one moment, these phantom soldiers are gone the next.

In April 1865, following final defeat, in the presence of Ulysses S. Grant, Robert E. Lee signed a document at Appomattox Court House surrendering his 1st Confederate Army. Towards the end of the month the 2nd Confederate Army also surrendered. The Union had been saved. In December the emancipation of slaves was announced and 4 million African Americans were freed, although freedom meant hard times were to come for many.

April 14th that same year had witnessed the assassination of President Abraham Lincoln by John Wilkes Booth at Ford's Theatre in Washington D.C. Lincoln had forseen his own death and had a premonition that he would not survive for long into his second term of office, to which he had been elected the previous month. His ghost has been seen quite frequently in a number of places including the White House itself, where several recent presidents have caught sight of him. And sometimes during the last week of April, his phantom funeral train, pulled by a shining new 1860s Union locomotive with nine Pullman cars draped in black, slowly railroads its way silently across the landscape carrying his mortal remains all the way from Washington to Springfield, Illinois with 300 mourners in attendance.

Gallant Animal Spirits

We must also remember the animals—horses, mules and wildlife that just happened to have their habitats in different places where fighting took place. Company C of the 8th Wisconsin Infantry Regiment had as their lucky mascot a bald eagle named 'Old Abe', acquired in 1861 when their Captain, John E. Perkins paid a trader $5 for the young bird, which had started life as the pet of a Chippewa chieftain. The Captain named him after President Abraham Lincoln and soon the men had built a hefty perch for their new recruit, painting it red, white and blue. That autumn the regiment went off to war, accompanied by Old Abe who proved an inspiring addition to the ranks.

At Farmington, Mississipi in the following

May, shells were bursting all around but Abe jumped off his perch, joining the men who were lying on the ground for cover. During an attack on Vicksburg a few weeks later Abe's handler, though uninjured, slipped and fell under fire. Nonetheless Abe, a powerful bird, pulled him—and the perch—into the shelter of a ravine nearby.

In the midst of battle Abe sometimes remained on his perch, screeching defiance at the enemy, miraculously unscathed by the bullets whistling past him, surviving over forty battles and skirmishes. On parade he would spread his seven-foot wing span, saluting the Company colours with a special ritualistic screech, knowing this would bring a reward from his high-ranking officers—a tot of brandy or Scotch whiskey.

A memorial to Old Abe, erected by the state of Wisconsin, now stands in the Vicksburg National Military Park. His six-foot bronze statue displayed on a high plinth impresses all who see it. And at full moon in late autumn and winter, many people claim to have seen Old Abe—or maybe his spirit—rising from his plinth to swoop, soar and screech high in the surrounding sky—the bald eagle, emblem of his country, still paying his respects to the colours of the United States of America.

INTERLUDE
'REST IN PEACE'

*'All that in this delightful garden grows
Should happy be, and have immortal bliss.'*

Edmund Spencer

Imagine walking through the sultry glades of a very special garden—the wonderful Bonaventure Cemetery—the Graveyard of Good Fortune. Set on the banks of St. Augustine Creek, Savannah, Georgia, USA it has been described as 'a venerable feast of the senses' with its fine, lush trees draped with Spanish moss and old, neglected shrubberies, ornamental ironwork and beautiful statuary.

The spirit of a Confederate soldier is said to guard this resting-place of dead comrades, although soldiers from the Spanish-American war and others who died in both world wars are also buried here. But there are other ghosts here of a different kind, bringing to this strange place of special beauty, a reminder that life is never far away.

The site, originally known as Bonaventure Plantation, was re-purchased by Josiah Tattnall some years following its confiscation from both his family and that of John

Mullryne, who had remained loyal to King George III during the American War of Independence in the second part of the 18th century. Since he was addicted to living the good life, Tattnall's reputation as the perfect host soon spread and many were the grand occasions at the plantation with guests arriving from far and wide. On one such night, due to the many candles used to light its rooms, the great mansion caught fire and the conflagration quickly spread. Tattnall, however, showed no sign of alarm but instructed his servants to transfer all the chairs—plus the table laden with exquisite food—onto the extensive lawn outside, where he encouraged the company to continue enjoying their dinner.

'May the joy of this occasion never end!' was the remarkable toast of one of the guests while the now insatiable flames consumed the mansion in record time, lighting up the night sky. Tattnall stood up to smash his goblet against a nearby oak in response to the toast, and all the other guests followed suit. (One wonders whether they had already drunk so much that they were incapable of appreciating the gravity of the situation). But the event passed into history and on warm autumn evenings, it seems that the party still continues at Bonaventure. Witnesses have heard lively chatter, hearty laughter, the clinking of cutlery and a myriad glasses being smashed in what can only be described as a truly absurd Monty Python style situation!

The Tattnalls were the first to be buried at Bonaventure during the early 19th century. Josiah himself followed his wife Harriet to the family plot, joining four of their children who had died young. When the city of Savannah later negotiated land deals, part of the old plantation became a public cemetery, and a further 60 hectares were purchased as recently as 1907. Now in the absence of the tense drama of battlefield, both the living and the dead find peace and repose amongst the lush vegetation and exotic flowers, many of which are also brought here in bunches or made into wreaths.

*   *   *

Flowers perform a very special function in any graveyard, whether as grand as Bonaventure or as humble as our nearest churchyard. Beautiful blossoms radiate a feeling of spiritual comfort and well-being, and though physically seeming to do nothing, they have long been recognised as working a gentle but powerfully essential magic of comfort and transformation—though ancient beliefs firmly suggest that to take a living flower from a grave can court disaster for the family of the person concerned, or his own death within the year.

There are many traditions regarding flowers. Red flowers have always been considered lucky, red being the colour of blood; and red poppies, so representative of the fallen throughout two World Wars, are symbolic of life itself. But to scatter the petals or leaves of a red rose on the ground is supposed to predict an early death—while white flowers on graves or in wreaths offer hope and consolation and the yellow of daffodils or chrysanthemums signify youth, concern and chivalry.

The Romans once scattered roses on their graves not only to signify the brevity of mortality, but also to acknowledge the possibility of continuing life in the beyond. It is the power and beauty of the rose more than any other flower—apart from the lotus—that has endorsed it a worthy symbol of birth, rebirth and the hope of eternal life. This is perhaps what other places of the dead as well as the Bonaventure Cemetery represent. And with its haunting eeriness and calm in dappled moon and sunlight, is it any wonder that the spirits of battle-weary men should choose to linger in what to them may be the nearest thing to Heaven?

'I sing of time trans-shifting, and I write
How roses first came red and lilacs white;
I write of groves, of twilights, and I sing
The Court of Mab, and of the Fairy King;

I write of hell; I sing (and ever shall)
Of heaven, and hope to have it after all.'

Robert Herrick

6
APOCALYPSE

'I snatched two poppies
From the parapet's ledge,
Two bright red poppies
That winked on the ledge.
Behind my ear
I stuck one through,
One blood red poppy
I gave to you.

The sandbags narrowed
And screwed out our jest,
And tore the poppy
You had on your breast . . .
Down—a shell—O! Christ,
I am choked . . . safe . . . dust blind, I
See trench floor poppies
Strewn. Smashed you lie.'

In the Trenches
Isaac Rosenberg

Protective angels, saints, even phantom English bowmen from the Battle of Agincourt (1415) were claimed to have been sighted during the Great War of 1914–1918 along with many other strange phenomena, and many people including the writer Vera Brittain, witnessed strange, long-remembered sunsets in that summer of 1914.

Such forebodings, from signs in the skies and phantom armies to all sorts of visions, have been recorded throughout history, many being mentioned in the Old Testament. In Roman times there was even a system whereby the result of an approaching battle (for example, Lake Regillus in 496 BC) was dependent on the appearance of the Divine Twins, Castor and Pollux, as two spectral horsemen. Other heavenly signs like eclipses, comets, thunder and lightning were also regarded as signs of ill-portent. The appearance of Halley's comet, for example was connected to the Battle of Hastings (1066) and the demise of Anglo-Saxon England.

At the start of hostilities in 1914 Britain, 'this Sceptred Isle' and heart of Empire, regarded herself as being militarily invincible, most definitely on the right side of any supernatural or divine intervention. Yet few realised that millions all over Europe would soon be caught up in the most savage and destructive drama the civilised world had ever experienced. For the first time, ordinary people and military personnel would be equally vulnerable in this hybrid war of traditional horse-drawn wagons, gun-carriages, cavalry charges; of gas, machine-guns, tanks and fighter planes, weapons of mass destruction and bombardment on a hitherto unknown scale.

Everything that had previously been considered good and permanent in life now seemed threatened. Many people were to feel that conventional religions had let them down—or conversely, were all those signs and portents an indication that the deity was making a determined stand and giving them much needed reassurance, after all?

These terrible uncertainties brought to the social psyche a more ready acceptance than normal of things supernatural and of myth. Whether made-up stories or facts, perhaps we should consider what Bronislaw Malinowski said in 1926;

> *'Myth fulfils . . . an indispensable function; it expresses, enhances and codifies belief; it safeguards and enhances morality; it vouches for the efficiency of ritual and contains practical rules for the guidance of man. Myth is a vital ingredient of human civilisation; it is not an idle tale, but a hard-worked active fact.'*

As a form of protection during the Great War, many soldiers carried lucky charms such as amulets, crucifixes and gemstones just as many of their modern counterparts do, today. Others kept a copy of Psalm 91 in their pockets, for this was to be regarded by many religious people as a holy war, the greatest significant event since Biblical times. So how did it start, such a terrible 'war to end all wars' which was also to initiate so many of its own myths and legends, so many strange sightings?

Into the Maelstrom

A series of treaties in place since the Franco-Prussian War (1870–71) had fettered Europe's strongest nations. One of two alliances had brought together Britain, France and Russia while the other paired Germany with the Austro-Hungarian Empire. Unease, hard feelings and suspicion had evolved over the years until with such fragmentation of trust, all that was needed was one event to set conflict into motion.

This finally came with the assassination of Archduke Franz Ferdinand, heir to the Austro-Hungarian Empire, while on a visit to the Bosnian capital of Sarajevo. Austria immediately accused the Serbs of this dastardly deed, threatening them with military action. The Serbs swiftly appealed to Russia for help and, becoming increasingly alarmed as Russia mobilised its army, Germany declared war on 1st August, 1914, thus dragging many other nations into the conflict.

The German generals needed a quick

victory over France before the Czar's army attacked from the east but the French had considerably strengthened their defences along their border with Germany. In order to bypass these defences and save time, the German forces needed to cross neutral Belgium instead and had initially asked for permission, which would have enabled them to enter France from the north. Belgium refused, and Britain threatened to enter the war if Belgium's neutrality was violated. It was. Germany, with no hesitation, swiftly occupied the country and on 4th August, Britain declared war on Germany. Now the maelstrom was to begin, brutally unstoppable, like some freak but terrible storm of nature.

The British Expeditionary Force (BEF) consisted of highly-trained, professional soldiers. During August 1914, while marching through Belgium, they unexpectedly came face-to-face with the main advance of the German Army at Mons, a mining town on marshy ground, criss-crossed by canals and littered with slag heaps. However, this was a place already steeped in folklore. It was here, according to the Belgians, that St. George killed the Dragon—and now the Dragon became synonymous with Kaiser Wilhelm II and his army as forces of evil to be overcome.

Greatly outnumbered, the British under attack fought back gallantly and ferociously, so much so that the Germans thought the BEF was much larger than it actually was—possibly because the British had fast-firing Lea Enfield rifles. As fighting continued however, (with heavy losses on both sides) it seemed that the Germans were threatening to outflank the British. Then suddenly, at around midnight— so it was claimed—a host of angels actually 'descended from Heaven, dressed as archers, and halted the Germans in their tracks.' This enabled the British to withdraw beneath the cover of darkness. Yet many British rank-and-file soldiers believed they had won, certain they had slowed down the German advance.

Starved of definite news about the war, journalists soon filled pages with accounts of the miraculous appearances of the angels of Mons. Meanwhile Arthur Machen of the London *Evening News*, finding the headlines depressing, had also created something he hoped would boost morale—his story 'The Bowmen' was about phantom English Bowmen of Agincourt coming to the rescue of the British forces.

Short stories previously published by the *Evening News* by various authors, including Machen himself, were certainly regarded as fiction. But in 'The Bowmen' the author skilfully weaved fact with fiction, so much so the general public became confused, especially as the same newspaper also reported that the BEF, so they believed, had only been saved from disaster by 'something miraculous'. Of course such 'comfort talk' was exactly what was needed.

Divine Intervention—or Devil's Work?

Machen was held responsible for creating the 'Bowmen' myth—but in fact the Bowmen, like the angels, were said to have been witnessed at least three weeks before the publication of his story. Rumours of dead German soldiers being found with no visible wounds were later also connected to Machen's story. Some had indeed been found with arrows in them, but not those of the phantom Bowmen of Agincourt. These were made of steel, aimed by French and British pilots (the latter members of the Royal Flying Corps, forerunners of the RAF) over the Western Front as early into the War as September 1914.

And exactly who had actually witnessed these Heavenly interventions? Evidence suggests that many sightings seemed to be second-hand, 'seen by a friend' or 'a friend of a friend' or 'by some officer'. Yet very interestingly, although a report from the German side after Mons insisted that no angels whatsoever were seen by them, there were seemingly contradictory reports from their cavalry. As they had charged towards the BEF, they became aware of a strange, invisible barrier, causing their terrified horses to pull up as suddenly as though at the edge of a precipice and then bolt. The conclusion was that the Germans thought the British had invented some 'devilish device'.

A certain Private J. East, from the Lincolnshire Regiment, was involved in street-fighting against the enemy as part of a rearguard action at Mons. He later described what appeared to be another sighting, claiming that as the Germans advanced towards his group of soldiers, his men witnessed ' . . . a long line of white forms, stretching from house to house' and believed 'that a white barricade had been sent by some unseen power to protect that small body of English.' A handful of wounded soldiers were said to have seen them also. Yet strangely, although mentioned for some years as part of Belgium's tourist information, nothing was officially reported at the time—though inevitably, word spread quickly about the angels of Mons throughout the British Army and beyond during the ensuing years of conflict.

In March 1915, during the fighting at Neuve-Chappelle, an advance by the British was checked by German machine-gun fire, the result being stalemate. One soldier later intimated that when they felt safe to do so, they eventually climbed out of the trenches and as they did so, he and his comrades actually saw 'the angels all around us.'

Many people were convinced that there would be large numbers of witnesses to such appearances, although in actual fact few reliable ones were produced. It was even rumoured that the War Office had placed a 'Silence Order' on them. But all the same many individuals who survived the hell of trench life and warfare, who also had lucky escapes from serious wounds or avoided being killed, became convinced—even those living into old age—that they had been protected by a guardian angel of Mons simply because they *had* survived.

The Living Dead

There are rational explanations that would put such stories down to acute exhaustion brought on by hours, days of intensive fighting, continuous deafening gunfire, the contagion of fear for life and limb, atrocious living conditions, as well as the ordeal of long route marches carrying heavy back packs in all weather conditions. Obviously, all these were bound to have a devastating effect on the minds of the men, resulting in the inevitable bending of the facts and distorting interpretations of whatever experiences actually befell them.

The battle zones were places only too suited

to phantom visions and ghastly hauntings. No Man's Land was described by David Clarke, author of *The Angel of Mons* as 'that eerie wasteland of craters, barbed wire and tree stumps that divided the Allied and German trenches'. This was where the living and the dead met and mingled, some soldiers believing that those killed still carried on fighting alongside them. It would not have been surprising, for their physical remains lay nearby in shallow, hastily-dug graves while some were even left exposed and rotting, even if temporarily, in the awful place. Old photographs of shell-shocked, exhausted soldiers sometimes even show human bones lining the trenches, while many of the injured said they were convinced they had been stretchered off the battlefield by their dead comrades. All sorts of things were seen under duress and it was *because* men were partially living in another dimension—a sort of 'reassurance zone'—that supernatural aid could well have manifested itself in some form or another.

Although the Government at the time may have officially denied the existence of the 'angel phenomenon', unofficially it could well have encouraged people's belief in them—as well as similar encouraging tales. Someone even composed the 'Angel of Mons Waltz', which was published as sheet music in London. There were piano pieces too, and the story was adapted for stage and film. The Church—perhaps naively—printed religious leaflets for distribution throughout the land and abroad. There were 'Angel of Mons' postcards. The artist Arthur Forrestier took Machen's 'Bowmen' story and produced his well-known and dramatic pen and ink drawing which was published in the *Illustrated London News*.

From a morale-boosting point-of-view, not only for the grimly traumatised soldiers bogged down in trench warfare but for the ordinary people back home, the idea that despite the current desperate war situation, there was divine or supernatural help and protection at hand (with an inevitable British victory implied as the outcome) had obvious advantages.

In such a desperate and prolonged conflict as the Great War, conditions were manifest for other unusual encounters besides the 'Angel Phenomenon'. For example, a regular officer told about the time a company of phantom soldiers had helped him and his men during a relentless attack. He was given the order to retreat from a particular trench they had been holding under difficult circumstances—while almost immediately a voice boomed from behind '*Don't* retreat!' Turning, he saw to his amazement an officer in khaki together with a large company of men. Almost simultaneously, he also noticed the Germans who had been attacking his force suddenly pull back, aghast!

A prisoner they later captured admitted they had been terrified by the 'ghost soldiers that had appeared out of nowhere'. Strangely, the British officer claimed he had known the 'ghost soldier' who had given him the order to 'stay put', recognising him as a Boer General in the Boer War. The puzzle was that they had then been on opposing sides—so why had this former foe chosen to come over to aid the British, at least for the moment, in this greater conflict?

*　　　*　　　*

Sudden moments of uncanny awareness happen to all of us, to a greater or lesser extent. Primarily, they can help ensure our very survival by enabling us to avoid some potentially threatening situation—a gift especially developed where animals are concerned, particularly in situations of stress. One soldier of some years' service in the Army once spoke of his incredible escape from an ambush while fighting in France. Making for the cover of a wood, he and his fellow cavalrymen were about to take a particular route when their horses suddenly stopped, refusing to go any further. As time was short and the company felt exposed, they chose another road nearby. Later they were to learn that a German ambush had been in wait had they gone via the original route.

At the start of hostilities, even the two eldest daughters of Czar Nicholas II—the Grand Duchesses Olga (19) and Tatiana (17)—who were working as nurses in field hospitals, wrote to friends in the British Red Cross concerning wounded soldiers who had experienced visions on the battlefield.

On the eastern front in mid-August 1914, the Germans were taken by surprise by the speed of Czar Nicholas II's forces as they bit deep into East Prussian territory, but at the Battle of Tannenberg a month later, they reacted against the hitherto victorious Russian army by slaughtering 30,000 of its men, capturing 90,000, while thousands more beat a quick retreat. Despite this setback, the Russian 2nd army under General Rennenkampf, was successful in occupying Austrian territory.

It was here, according to reports, that the Russian troops were overwhelmingly inspired by the spectral appearance in white uniform, and mounted on a great white horse, of the legendary General Skobeleff, hero of the 1877–78 Russo-Turkish War. Like St George to the British, so the General's ghost was said to appear whenever the Russian troops were under dire threat.

On the eve of the Battle of Augustova (1st October, 1914) while many Russian troops prayed for a victorious outcome, a vision in the sky was said to have been seen by thousands. It appeared to be of the Virgin Mary, pointing westward whilst holding the Infant Jesus. Awestruck, the soldiers fell to their knees in worship and as the vision faded, it assumed the shape of a cross. Yet despite their initial success in the Great War, the Russian Army would soon taste the bitterness of defeat in spite of the encouragement of supposed Divine Guidance. Later, as the machinery of Revolution gathered pace, many thousands of her troops, beaten and starving, needed little persuasion to desert the doomed cause of their Czar Nicholas II, for a promised Utopia which in the final instance would prove to be equally as doomed.

Strangely, of all the visions experienced by soldiers of many nations during the Great War—whether the result of mass hysteria or by wildfire rumour—none seemed to have had quite the same effect as the angels of Mons phenomenon on Great Britain and her Empire. Perhaps though not officially admitting to its existence, Britannia might quietly have approved of it after all.

7
'KEEP THE HOME FIRES BURNING'

'East and west on fields forgotten
Bleach the bones of comrades slain,
Lovely lads and dead and rotten;
None that go return again.'

on the idle hills of summer
A. E. Housman

Prospects of war often brew a fervour of nationalistic pride on the larger part of a country's population; while deeper thoughts, sometimes assailed by strange dreams, apparitions and a sense of foreboding has usually been the lot of the few. What made the prospect of the 1914–18 war seem different to many was the true envisaged scale of the conflict. There was a feeling of *immense* foreboding everywhere.

But once war had been declared, thousands of men, many poorly paid in heavy, dangerous industries like iron and steel making, quarrying and in the coal-mines, fervently took the King's shilling to enter the colours with prospects of better pay and adventure. They would soon put the enemy back where they belonged. 'It'll all be over by Christmas!' was the cry—though soon would be heard the

123

mournful echo of cries of a far different kind.

In the simple words of *'on the idle hills of summer'* Housman ingeniously conveys with intense poignancy within the text of pastoral landscape, a premonition of the cruel aftermath of war with its wasteful sacrifice of young lives upon the battlefield. But in penning that last haunting line, the poet obviously preferred not to take into account the latent possibilities of the supernatural. Do they really *all* never return? Perhaps that is not quite correct for there seem to have been reports of many phantom 'soldiers from the wars returning'.

During the Great War, for example, it is said that one dark night a phantom soldier on sentry duty halted an ambulance (location not specified) and vanished when the driver got out. Ahead was a gaping hole in the road. Without a warning from the spectral sentry, there might have been a serious accident.

The ghost of a khaki-clad soldier from the same period, bare-headed and mud-stained, has certainly been seen in Westminster Abbey. Standing near to the tomb of the Unknown Warrior, might this be the spirit of that Unknown Warrior himself? Or is it some other unknown who had regularly worshipped here or even sung in the choir? Perhaps more simply it is the spirit of a long-dead soldier paying his respects to an old war-time pal.

Some spectral soldiers are believed to

return if only fleetingly. Among the many ghosts which have been experienced at the Theatre Royal, Winchester one in particular was seen there during the Great War—of the former lighting man who had left for active service at the Front. During a performance of *Soldiers of the King* one of the cast fainted dramatically on stage and on recovering, said she had seen the lighting man standing in the wings in his uniform, even though it was known he was away fighting for his country. Next day, a War Office telegram arrived for his mother saying he had been killed in action.

*　　　*　　　*

So many people are affected by war and not necessarily on the battle front. Close relatives—parents, wives, sweethearts, brothers, sisters, even cousins of those who have gone 'off to the fray' and are perhaps many hundreds of miles from home—know little of whether their dear ones are alive or dead, especially if the official report says simply 'missing'. Living in a sort of limbo, they hope and pray that their particular soldier will, after all, come through safely for then as now, family bonds—of love, respect, or even of quarrelsome disagreement—still hold fast.

Is it any wonder that many 'dead' soldiers return, appearing in familiar three-dimensional physical form or even via dreams, to tell relatives that although they have left this 'mortal coil' all is well with them. Some particularly wanted to convey their relief—even joy—at having escaped from the man-made hell of which they had been a part. Certain individuals have also been known to appear whilst fully alive, but when experiencing some acute moment of danger—only later has it been discovered that they managed to come through safely. Where death *has* occurred (though with exceptions) they have often appeared to their loved ones from twelve hours down to within only a few seconds after death, distance being no barrier.

One of the most well known wartime examples was that of the poet Wilfred Owen, who appeared after his death just a week before the end of the Great War. The visitation was to his brother Harold, far away on board ship at the time, who later wrote about the experience:

> *'He did not speak, only smiled his most gentle smile . . . I felt terribly tired and I lay down; instantly I went into a deep, oblivious sleep. When I woke up, I knew with absolute certainty that Wilfred was dead.'*

It was discovered that Wilfred Owen was seen by his brother within seconds following his death, which was due to a sniper's bullet to the head during a lull in the fighting.

Another example came from two sisters, Agnes Ray and Ethel Gorton, originally brought up by their grandmother in Silverdale, Newcastle-under-Lyme. All their lives they had been very psychic and telepathic, so they told David Bell, author of *Ghosts & Legends of Staffordshire & The Black Country*. Even though Agnes now lives in Falkirk and Ethel in Stoke-on-Trent, each knows what the other is doing, even though they are both separated by hundreds of miles.

On an occasion during the Great War their grandmother, then a young woman, was working in the kitchen when she was suddenly aware of someone standing behind her. She turned and saw that it was her son Jim, then in his early twenties and home on leave from the army—or so she thought.

'Mother,' he said, affectionately. He broke the news that he had passed over, she was not to touch him, but to expect something in the post. 'Forget me not!' he finally added, before disappearing.

Next day the dreaded news arrived that Jim had been gassed. The day following, a small package arrived. It was from Jim, as he had promised. On opening it the girls' grandmother found it was a small, golden heart engraved with the words 'Mother— forget me not' on a chain. Agnes and Ethel recalled how on every Poppy Day after, their

127

grandmother would wear it. Furthermore they said that although they never knew their Uncle Jim, they remember feeling his presence around the house. There was also a small organ that only he used to play. Fascinatingly, when either Agnes or Ethel was alone in the house, the organ was heard being played.

Going Home

Sometimes this kind of recollection can be even more puzzling and intriguing—often difficult to interpret. Another I encountered during my research work concerned Harriet Laurent of Sturgeon Bay, Wisconsin. She wrote about the time her mother received a letter postmarked France, from Tom, her eldest son. In it he said he was coming home on leave and one morning in July 1918, he entered the house, carrying his duffle-bag.

'Mother, I'm home!' he said with a radiant smile.

Overjoyed, she rushed forward to embrace him—and he just disappeared. Suddenly heartbroken, she just knew that he was dead. A few days later this was confirmed. The telegram said that Tom had been killed in action.

When twelve months later, Harriet's father was taken gravely ill Tom appeared again. Her mother saw him enter the house once more with his duffle-bag.

'I'm sorry,' he said quietly, before vanishing. That night, Harriet's father died.

Three months later, her young brother suffered convulsions and for a third time her mother saw Tom enter the house. She knew her youngest child would die—and so he did that evening. By the time Harriet wrote of these events, her mother was in her early eighties and she could not help but wonder whether the next time Tom appeared, he would he be taking *her* with him. A dubious prospect indeed for the family, though for her mother, the thought of being reunited with her son could well have been a source of comfort.

*   *   *

Another touching story happened shortly before the Armistice in November, 1918, when one of Eileen Hart Prentiss's brothers was due home on leave in Loraine, Ohio.

It was a cold night, there had been a light snowfall outside, and she and her mother had gone to bed. Later they were woken up by the growls of their terrier dog, which always spent the night downstairs on a chair beneath a front window. The front door was heard creaking open and footsteps then started up the stairs. Immediately Eileen's mother went out onto the landing, they stopped and there seemed to

129

be no-one there. She called a neighbour, whose light she could see was still on and another neighbour also came from across the street. The dog was still growling as she normally did if there were strangers around.

On checking, it was found that all doors and windows were locked from the inside, Eileen's mother especially remembering she had locked the front door before retiring for the night. With all rooms checked, it was obvious that no-one had actually come into the house apart from the neighbours and there were no other footprints in the snow outside. Then, suddenly, the neighbour from across the street recalled that just before he came over, he had seen the figure of a young soldier enter the house through the front door and thought nothing of it, assuming it was one of Eileen's brothers arriving home on leave.

Eileen's mother must have been beside herself with worry, doubtless assuming the 'visitor by night' could have been the spirit of a member of her family who had been injured or killed. But in fact this was not so. Just before the Armistice three weeks later, they received news that a young man who had lived at the house before Eileen's mother had bought it had been killed in France—the day before they had the visit from the phantom soldier.

There have even been instances where soldiers away at some theatre of war have felt convinced that the spirits of family members at home reversed the trend by contacting them— often as a warning just moments prior to mortal danger.

While Cordelia Sydney and Mary, her invalid sister, stayed at home with their mother, the girls' two brothers Jim and Jerry were serving in the Canadian Army. Because of his wounds, Jim had had a leg amputated while meanwhile, in May 1917, Jerry was fighting in France. One morning, he and two companions were walking through the forest to get much-needed rations to bring back to camp. Although exhausted after days of continual engagement with the enemy, they chatted about where they came from and about their folks back home. Then suddenly Jerry saw Mary, his invalid sister, standing in front of him. Quickly, she bent down and undid his bootlaces. Slightly confused, he moved forward and stumbled—and in less than two seconds, his two companions were riddled with machine-gun bullets. Jerry realised that had it not been for Mary he, too, would have died instantly.

A month later, his company having been involved in another exhausting period of military engagement, Jerry woke up one morning thinking he could hear Mary urging him to get up quickly. Imagining he must be dreaming, he nearly turned over to go back to sleep but he heard Mary's message again, this time with much more urgency. It was very strange, he thought, realising that his invalid sister was unable to speak! Then came her final, desperate plea for Jerry to get up and this time he roused himself, leaving his tent and moving away from the camp double-quick. Just then his tent, with all the others, was hit by a shell and presently, when he was able to return to the camp, Jerry was to find that all his army pals, tents and equipment had been blown to pieces.

A few weeks later, still very shocked, Jerry went to see his brother Jim, who was convalescing in London. It was there that he learned that their sister Mary, back in Canada, had died. She had made their mother understand that she felt instinctively that Jerry was in great danger and that he needed her and that she was going to die to save him.

*   *   *

Inevitably in war, all sorts of people perish— young, old, the good-and-gifted, the not-so-good and the downright despicable. Through war too, others survive sometimes deplorable experiences created by others. While some, far away from the fighting, shall we say, create their own skull-duggery in the belief that 'the dead shall never know'.

Jim Daniel of West Virginia joined up in 1917, leaving behind Darlene, the girl of his dreams. He was one of the first American soldiers to arrive on French soil when the United States joined the European Allies in a final push to defeat Germany. Jim's letters to Darlene were to arrive frequently back in Virginia but his elder brother Will had also become infatuated with Darlene, and he began to intercept Jim's letters to her. As a result, she grew very worried about his safety and eventually, Will faked a telegram with the news that Jim had been killed in action.

A heartbroken Darlene turned to Will and his concern and feelings of affection towards her, and in October of that year they were married. On Christmas Eve, while in the kitchen preparing supper, Darlene thought she heard the front door open and then was aware of someone conversing urgently in the living room with her husband Will. With a chill, she realised it was Jim's voice!

'I know what you've done to Darlene and me,' he said. 'And I've come to kill you!'

Not knowing what to think, Darlene stood rooted to the spot. She could not move until a loud gunshot rang out, and on rushing into the living room, she glimpsed the vague form of a soldier about to disappear through the door.

Will lay on the floor, shot through the forehead, an expression of utter disbelief still on his face. Darlene just stood, transfixed by the terrible scene for what she later believed was a long time, until she was roused by loud knocking on the front door. When she managed to go to open it, a boy handed her a telegram from the War Department. It read; 'To William Daniel: Regret to inform you that on December 21st 1917 your brother James Daniel was killed in action in Germany.'

Will's murderer was never caught, despite exhaustive police enquiries. The telegram boy had been the only visitor that Christmas Eve. No gun was ever discovered and Jim had never personally owned one. Darlene was adamant that it was Jim's ghost that had returned home to West Virginia, to seek revenge for Will's wrong-doings.

Such stories may be interpreted as bizarre, sometimes even sinister. Each is typical yet untypical, uniquely individual in its own way, indicating that in certain situations, spirits appear to have the will and the way of communicating with those who were nearest— most loved or hated even—when that person was living. Such private dramas may seem small when compared to the larger epics of the battlefield, but it is these stories, making up the huge human impact of individual emotions, that really overwhelm us in stories of war.

As an historic footnote: in 1918, when negotiating for peace, the American President Woodrow Wilson put forward demands that the Germans surrender all gains in Russia and Romania; in the West, that Alsace-Lorraine be surrendered and Belgium be evacuated, together with masses of arms to be cleared from these countries—and from France—within fourteen days. Also under the Wilson Plan Germany's navy was to be rendered ineffective. Meanwhile, Lloyd George, the British Prime Minister, and Clemenceau, his French counterpart, also demanded financial reparation for all war damage suffered by the Allies.

So for Germany, by way of the Treaty of Versailles, the 'end of hostilities' was at the high price of near bankruptcy and such humiliating terms persuaded many—even at the time—that the Allies had merely gained some twenty years of peace. The uneasy ghosts were still restless. Already the Great War, the 'war to end all wars' was being referred to as World War One, and it left a world so haunted that its successor would bring even more bloodshed and call into being ghosts of its own.

8

IN GHOSTLY RANKS

'For me there was nothing left but rubble and the ghosts.'

Heinz, former WW2 German soldier

The Treaty of Versailles of 1919 had been a unique opportunity for the lasting peace of which all nations had been dreaming by the end of World War One. Yet through lack of foresight on the part of many politicians its terms actually contributed to the inevitable melting-pot of what was to become World War Two. The League of Nations, formed the following year, enabled countries to settle their grievances around the negotiating table yet practically, it lacked punch. It preached disarmament, but with no means of enforcing it. Disgruntled, some countries resigned to go their own way while the Allies (Great Britain, France, USA, and others) felt satisfied that Germany had been sufficiently 'reined in' for the time being. But finding a situation where it was unable to move forward, Germany itself felt angered, embittered not only at the reparation it had had to pay but at territory forfeited under the terms of the Treaty.

Once elected Chancellor in 1933, Adolf

Hitler galvanised a wounded nation towards nationalistic pride once more. Many in the new hierarchy who had been involved in the Great War had taken to heart the ignoble conditions for Germany's surrender. Now she moved forward again domestically and internationally beneath the sign of the swastika. She began to re-arm and on 1st September 1939, Hitler invaded Poland. In support of the Poles, Britain and France declared war on Germany two days later

When it came, many believed this renewed aggression was Hitler's own personal revenge—his advance was always fast, hoping to catch any opposition on the wrong foot. In terms of human and material destruction, this war was to be even more horrendous than World War One. Much more mobile and fast moving, over fifty million people, so it is estimated, were lost in the conflict that would eventually end in Nazi Germany's total defeat.

In the Far East Imperial Japan had already made inroads into Korea, China and Manchuria. Their military expansion added to the horrors of the maelstrom, signifying as it did vast movements of armies, prisoners-of-war, 'undesirables' transported to death-camps, and swathes of fleeing refugees; emotions of acute fear, mistrust and the terrors of death surged throughout this huge 1939–1945 Arena of War. Mobilisation on both sides proved to be on a previously unimagined scale.

Thus conditions were once again ripe for that alternative reality to gather strength once more—for the paranormal, to some always that inexplicable 'reassurance zone'—to seep inevitably into many aspects of the conflict. Strange events were to occur of both reassurance and of amazement.

A Phantom Plane Flies

One night in November 1942, RAF Fairlop in Essex went on full alert. From Control Tower it was reported that an unidentified plane was approaching. All spitfires of No. 603 Squadron were grounded, so instinctively everyone knew it had to be a German aircraft. As it approached, searchlights swept the sky and the ack-ack battery opened fire. But almost immediately a cease-fire was ordered. The searchlights had revealed an old bi-plane which appeared to have mysteriously flown through the hail of bullets completely unscathed. For several seconds it remained in view—long enough to be identified before disappearing again—and revealed itself as one of the most effective planes ever to have flown during the Great War, a Sopwith Camelfighter.

Apparently a squadron of Sopwiths had been based at Hainault Farm, the former name of RAF Fairlop, and flown against attacks both by German Gotha aircraft and Zeppelins, some of them being specially adapted for night use. Ultimately, this spectral return of a World War One aircraft became legendary throughout the entire RAF.

Inevitably throughout World War Two, people, particularly those in the services, were always on the move. There were many boarding houses scattered throughout England where service personnel were billeted. Such a one was on the south coast, with soldiers coming and going at all hours, according to a report by psychic researcher John Langston Davies.

One morning the landlady encountered a young blond soldier who handed her a green parcel, asking her to post it to his wife, which she agreed to do. Only later did she realise there was no forwarding address, so she opened it to find it contained just a few civilian clothes. She put the parcel aside assuming the soldier would get in touch, but he did not.

One day after the war, having just returned from doing some shopping, she was surprised to glimpse the young soldier on the stairs, carrying a green parcel. She asked her daughter about the visitor—the answer was that there had been no-one in the house except herself. Nonetheless the landlady fully expected to find the parcel gone but strangely, it was still in the cupboard where she had originally put it.

A more thorough search of the clothing revealed a wedding photograph in a coat pocket, and she recognised the bridegroom—it was the blond soldier. There was both a number and address of the photographer on the back, so the landlady wrote requesting the address of the couple. In due course she was able to post the parcel and ultimately received a letter from the soldier's wife thanking her, adding that she had been expecting it for some time. It had contained money for their baby, which had been concealed in one of the shoes in the parcel—her husband, she added, had died at Dunkirk in 1940.

This was the time when troops of the British Expeditionary Force retreating from France found themselves trapped on the beaches, being fired on and dive-bombed by the ruthless German war-machine. That so many were saved was due to the French First Army which managed to contain seven German divisions for four days. Almost 339,000 Allied troops were evacuated to Britain, some forty per cent of which were French. 800 vessels were involved, including all available civilian passenger ferries.

Under such dire, wartime conditions it was not surprising that many individuals claimed to have all sorts of premonitions, whether of a trivial nature or of far more significance. One such incident occurred to Commander George Potter in the early 1940s, when Egypt was providing a vital foothold for the British against Rommel's Afrika Korps in the North Africa Campaign. One of the British priorities was to maintain the bombing of Mediterranean shipping lanes along which enemy shipping supplied much-needed arms for the German troops.

One evening, Commander George Potter and Flight Officer Reg Lamb were enjoying a drink in the Officers' Mess. The atmosphere was noisy and lively, thanks mainly to a group of fellow officers on the other side of the room.

When Potter happened to glance across at them, he saw a very disturbing image that seemed to be superimposed onto another member of the company, Wing Commander Roy. For just a second, he could see only his friend's head, fixed in a strange and ghastly expression: from the shoulders down, the rest of his figure was shrouded in blackness. Troubled by Potter's sudden silence, Lamb asked whether he was all right, and Potter recounted what he had seen. Neither of them understood what it might mean, but they decided to say nothing to Wing Commander Roy for fear of upsetting him.

The following night, Commander Roy and his crew set out on a bombing mission. It was reported later that their plane had come down in the sea, although Potter and Lamb were relieved to hear that the crew had managed to board a life raft. Eventually however, they received news that Roy had actually drowned—and it was only then that Potter realised the significance of what he had seen in the Officers' Mess. It had been the dead Commander floating in the dark water wearing his lifebelt—a vision of what would happen to him, a ghost of the future.

Whether we believe in God, angels (not always with wings), saints or the spirits of loved ones on 'the other side of the moonlit door', it is in circumstances of acute fear that we may ask (even unconsciously) for protection from one or other such source of powerful energy.

Looking back, American Marvin Goodman believed it was a guardian angel or avatar that got him and his army pal through a potentially dangerous situation when they were stationed in Europe in 1945. By then the Allies had advanced into Germany, and the situation was very dangerous because they often had to rely on what might prove to be inaccurate information concerning enemy troop and gun placements. Given a map of the Darmstadt area, Goodman and his driver PFC Cain had orders to set out in their four-by-four truck and trailer to deliver supplies of small carbine rifles to variously-placed US contingents.

'This area is under enemy surveillance. Keep moving!' warned many road signs along the way. But along one road they had to travel, there were no such directives and Goodman and Cain began to feel 'edgy', crossing flat, exposed terrain as they headed towards a steep hill. Then out of nowhere, a GI appeared on the driver's side. Surprised and relieved, Cain pulled up.

'Hey, pal!' he called. 'Are we heading for the tank division of the Twelfth Army Group?'

The GI, calmly seating himself on the ground, replied: 'Go over the top of that hill and you'll probably not make it. There's a German 88 up there, blowing off everything it can!'

Shaken, Goodman shouted to Cain to turn the vehicle round and get the hell out of it. As the vehicle did so, Goodman leaned forward to say 'Thanks!' to their informant but found there was no sign of him. He had completely disappeared. The ground was flat and open, and there was nowhere to hide, neither could he have ran off. Goodman even wondered if he had been a German soldier dressed in American drabs—but if so, they could have both been taken prisoner or shot on the spot. It was then that Goodman realised this had been a guardian angel.

Spectral Warriors

In some cultures omens traditionally go hand-in-hand with powerful superstition—the coming of some major event may be recognised by a whole community, perhaps by paranormal means, or by more natural occurrences such as eclipses, shooting stars, the stages of the moon. A phantom army of Hawaiian warriors, its origin lost in ancient times, is said to march at night whenever something of great significance is about to happen. Near the village of Maluhonua, close to Pearl Habor, puzzled residents were woken on one very significant occasion by the sounds of marching feet, ancient chants and fierce drumming. Although there was no visible sign of anything, they identified the activity as coming from the ruins (heiau) of a nearby ancient temple before the invisible army actually marched through the village itself and then headed out to sea.

Simultaneously, marching feet were heard on the island of Kauai where much to the islanders' foreboding, they actually saw the ghostly warriors. It is said that these two

144

phantom armies marched just two hours before the devastating Japanese air attack on the US Pacific Fleet anchored in Pearl Harbor, early on the morning of Sunday 7th December, 1941.

Although the United States were already supplying Great Britain with arms against what seemed like overwhelming German odds, from that terrible day on, in which 2,400 Americans were killed and 1,178 wounded, she was very much involved in World War Two herself.

*   *   *

Bolstered by their swift success at Pearl Harbor, having temporarily crippled the US Pacific Fleet, the Japanese felt able to maintain a swift initiative. By the summer of 1942 as in Europe and the Atlantic Ocean, the continent of Asia and the Pacific Ocean had fallen deeply beneath the grip of war. Comrades at arms on both sides operated far from home, dying or surviving in horrific circumstances, continuing to experience those unforeseen moments of greatest danger.

In 1941, after serving with Sergeant Fred Miller, whom he never saw again, Herbert Smith of the 31st Infantry left Manila on a transfer back to the States. Some years later he returned to the Far East as a platoon leader in Okinawa, where the Japanese were putting up tough resistance. During a patrol their advance was halted by heavy machine-gun fire coming from a concealed vantage point ahead. Telling his patrol to wait, Herbert went on, crawling along the jungle floor for a bearing on the enemy's position.

'Hold on, Herb!' whispered a familiar voice.

Herbert stopped dead, scared not so much of the Japanese somewhere close to him, but by the fact that he was actually completely alone. Just then a shell exploded some fifty yards ahead. With the searing rasp of red-hot shrapnel all around, he pressed himself hard into the earth behind a small boulder. Had he continued to crawl forward, he would have been just one more fatality of the war. Returning to base with his platoon, he quietly thanked the familiar voice—that of his former Sergeant Fred Miller. But Herbert later learned that his old friend had been killed in action back in March 1942, against a Banzai charge on Bataan.

The Sign of White Heather

Individuals have claimed that they have received vitally important information during a crisis by the appearance of some person they had never previously met. Another kind of guardian angel, possibly.

Following the German invasion of France in

1940 a French lady, Madame Marguerite, had been forced to surrender most of her possessions including the family castle and estate to the enemy. Living in a tiny cottage on the edge of the estate with her young son and an elderly servant, she chose not only to remain to uphold the honour of her proud family, but also to defy the presence of arrogant German soldiers who despised her.

Her husband, away at war, was a descendant of Robert I of Scotland ('Robert the Bruce') whose portrait hung in the castle. It showed the King to have had bright red hair and a powerful chin—a man apparently who had had a quick temper. For many years white heather had featured prominently in the castle garden, and indeed, a sprig of that same heather appeared not only on the King's royal coat-of-arms but also on the emblem belonging to the nearby French city of Bruz.

One night, after putting her young son to bed, Madame Marguerite sat alone in the flickering candlelight, upset at not knowing whether her husband was alive or dead. Eventually, she went into an uneasy sleep. Later, waking up with a start, she knew she was no longer on her own. Dressed in armour, a tall, broad-shouldered figure stood before her, leaning on his sword. Madame Marguerite, although surprised, was unafraid, and was in fact much comforted.

'These are such dreadful times, Messire

Robert,' she sighed, recognising the King from his portrait in the castle.

'Indeed so, Madame Marguerite,' he responded. 'I have come to warn you, but do not be afraid. Soon the enemy will be vanquished. You see! But there will be utter devastation and when you see my sign, you must take your young son and elderly servant and flee from here!'

'But how will I know when?'

'At the sign of the Bruce,' he replied.

Madame Marguerite blinked—and she was alone again.

Had Robert the Bruce actually appeared to her, she wondered? Or had he been but part of some wishful dream?

Did it matter which? She certainly waited weeks for some sort of sign, despite Hitler's boast about the 'impregnability of Europe'—a statement soon to be challenged by gathering Allied action. Then one bright morning in May, with an unexplained sense of urgency and running the risk of more humiliation from the occupying arrogant Nazi soldiers, Madame Marguerite, with head held high, walked proudly into the garden that surrounded the castle. To her amazement, what greeted her was the actual sign she had been waiting for— that of 'the Bruce'—the white heather in full flower.

Instinctively she knew it was time to go. Taking her young son and the aged servant, they escaped, walking several miles to a convent where the sisters took them in. That night the city of Bruz was heavily bombed by Allied planes, the flames rising to over thirty feet. Many of the Germans there were killed, alongside those who had been occupying the family castle, which was also destroyed.

Following the Normandy Landings in June 1944, fighting was to continue for almost another year. Among those who arrived to liberate France, as it turned out, was the husband of Lady Marguerite. Although their castle had gone, somehow it no longer mattered. The couple were happy despite great losses, and like thousands of others, survived to rebuild their shattered lives.

*   *   *

Corporal Dee McNerful was one of many soldiers who did not survive. But Harry Beckelman, a fellow American Marine, remembered his death for more than the usual reasons. This was on the Pacific island of Guam in 1944, where the US Marines had just completed one of the fiercest campaigns of the War against the Japanese. Afterwards, Harry and Corporal McNerful were caring for the injured and dying when a sniper suddenly revealed himself and fired. McNerful fell, mortally wounded and in a flash, Harry killed the sniper.

After checking the sniper was really dead, he laid aside his carbine, knelt by the corporal, removed his helmet, then cradled his head. With his free hand he felt his pulse. When Harry raised him gently into a sitting position, his pulse faltered then stopped. Harry had seen many things concerning the dead and dying during his time as a marine, but nothing like the vision he was about to witness after Corporal McNerful had died in his arms. He saw what he could only describe as an uncanny sort of thick mist rising from the face of his comrade into the bright sunlight. As it did so, a beautiful rainbow formed within the mist, briefly displaying all the colours of the spectrum. A few seconds later it had gone. And ever since, Harry wondered if that rainbow was actually Corporal Dee McNerful's spirit leaving his body.

9
PSYCHIC ECHOES

*'The glamour gone, some scattered graves
  and memories dim remain:*
*With his old pals across the field, he'll never
  trek again;*
*But yet there's nothing he regrets as he
  awaits his Call,*
*For what was done or lost or won, he did
  his bit—that's all.'*

Untitled
Sergeant 4486

So those old battlefields may still vibrate with the actions of heroism, or brood in the dark colours of brute force and negative feeling, continuing to experience awesome spectral activity of once powerful opposing forces. 'Echoes' or time-slips of men and machinery on their way to a scene of conflict, actually engaged in the fighting or in piteous retreat have often been glimpsed on historic sites, and the psychic action that lingered from World War Two was far from being an exception.

What we actually see and hear may be perfectly logical according to the ways of the supernatural, but seem erratic and illogical to witnesses. For no-one will ever fully understand the ways of the supernatural.

It was in August 1951 that Mrs Dorothy Norton and her sister-in-law Miss Agnes Norton were enjoying a short holiday at Puys, a few miles from Dieppe on the Northern French coast. In the early hours of 4th August, they were both woken up by what they thought at first was the roar of an approaching storm coming in from the sea. Gradually, however, the noise increased to such intensity that the two ladies went out onto their balcony to see what was going on. By way of the street-lighting they could see the town and beach below. It was then that they realised there was no wind blowing. All appeared to be perfectly normal.

As the noise further increased and having both experienced the London Blitz, only a few years before, they were able to identify individual sounds within the cacophony—heavy gunfire, shells and mortar bombs exploding, the rumbling and droning of planes, the seemingly ever intensifying scream of dive-bombers; and amid all this, shouting and desperate cries for help. It seemed the whole area was now under attack—and yet the two ladies could see no fires, no bombs exploding, nor damage to any buildings in the town. Even the street-lamps refused to flicker. Occasionally, the sounds became less, sometimes even fading altogether for short intervals only to resume with renewed intensity. As dawn approached everything

152

slowly quietened and as the birds started to sing, the noise had ceased altogether.

What puzzled the two holidaymakers the next day was that everyone else in the house had slept quite undisturbed, despite the intensity of the noise. Discussing it with some French neighbours, they realised that back in August 1942 it was at Puys, Dieppe, Berneval and Pointe D'Ally that the British had attempted landings under the cover of darkness. The element of surprise was wiped out as they ran into a German coastal convoy. Fierce firing ensued, the landings being somewhat delayed. Enemy coastal defences had been alerted and heavy, unremitting bombardment was centred on the men in the landing craft. Eventually, landings were made at Dieppe (the main goal) while others tried to secure Pourville and Varengeville.

Waves of German aircraft were called in, counteracted by later help from the RAF, which attacked German coastal installations in the wake of earlier support that had run low on fuel and ammunition. Eventually, the members of the Royal Canadian Regiment who had managed to land at Puys surrendered, having found themselves trapped. Meanwhile, a small number of officers and men (some wounded) were evacuated from the beaches by British ships, while nearly 300 men were taken prisoner by the Germans. Other objectives in the campaign faired slightly better where the

British and Canadians were concerned, but the entire operation had ceased by 0900 hours, the next day.

What the ladies had experienced was an entire, faithful aural re-run of that doomed operation almost exactly nine years after the event—but not quite. So, why nine years? And why was their encounter on the 4th August 1951—the actual episode having occurred on 19th August 1942? Again, why aurally as opposed to also being visual? These are some of the mysteries about the psychic world that will probably never be understood.

Taking his dog for a walk early one Sunday morning in May in Portland, Dorset John Murphy casually looked down from the public gardens onto the deserted road below. Next moment, he sensed loud, frenzied activity as a line of American army trucks and tanks suddenly appeared and rattled to a halt. As some GIs in olive drab leaned against the vehicles, small tents were busily being pitched alongside the road. Other soldiers relaxing over coffee and cigarettes laughed and called to one another. Then the entire scene faded. Although this was in May 1976, John knew well what he had witnessed—a phantom re-enactment of American troops who had passed that way, en route to some secret D-Day embarkation point in May 1944.

Once at home, he excitedly described what he had seen to his wife Doreen. However, she suggested the whole thing could have been in his mind, especially as he was writing a book about the American forces coming to England to prepare for the Normandy landings ('Operation Overlord'). With a sigh, John admitted this might have been so—until the following Sunday morning. Out again bright and early, he went again to the same area, but this time he was armed with a tape recorder. Switching on, he sat and enjoyed what only seemed to be beautiful birdsong. Then over breakfast, John and Doreen listened attentively to the recording, especially when there was a strange 'click' and the raucous sounds of heavy engines, roaring of trucks, tanks and jeeps were heard.

'Here we go!' some guy shouted with an American accent.

As the sounds continued, John hastily called his teenage daughter to hear the recording.

But strangely, after the tape had been played a few times, the voice faded. By the time the local priest was invited to listen, he only heard the other sounds of activity. Eventually, these too were to fade. Twelve months later, in May 1977, John returned to the locality again with his tape recorder, but he never picked up any further sounds, nor encountered a repeat of the spectral happening.

Another of many intriguing psychic 'memories of war' is claimed to have occurred one summer day in 1979. The *Mainichi Daily News*, one of Japan's largest newspapers, received a phone-call from a highly stressed Mrs Ikeda, the owner of a local restaurant. Taking a short cut home through the grounds of the well known Inari Shrine in the Shinagawa district of Tokyo, she said she had encountered soldiers in combats, with rifles, and carrying flags of the Rising Sun.

'Then they just vanished into thin air,' she said.

Shortly afterwards, the Tokyo police received an anonymous call from a man which was traced to a public phone booth, near to the same Inari Shrine.

'Soldiers are walking around in the grounds,' came the information. 'Japanese Imperial soldiers. I should know because I was in the Army once.' Then he hung up.

The Inari Shrine was where young soldiers in World War Two would gather for prayers before being sent overseas to fight. If they were killed in action, it is said that their souls returned to one of Tokyo's other shrines—the Yasukuni—where, enshrined, are all the Japanese war heroes worshipped for their bravery achieved in combat.

Similarly, the Kamikaze pilots who volunteered for suicide missions to crash their planes into enemy warships, prepared themselves in a ritual of prayers and farewells, wearing the hachimaki, a white cloth tied around the forehead, decorated with poetic calligraphy and the symbol of the Rising Sun.

Several days after the reputed sightings, the team of caretakers at the Inari Shrine were tidying up when one of them discovered a World War Two army bayonet hidden in one of the stone lanterns. Some people later suggested it was hidden by a member of the Japanese Imperial Army years ago. If this was so, why did the weapon have no rust?

Traitor's Revenge

A psychic echo or 'memory of war' can stretch the very bounds of credulity. The late summer of 1951 saw John Allen arrive at Calais from England, hoping to do a cycling tour of France. He neared Anger in Brittany, in heavy rain—then he had a puncture. With no spare inner tube, he tried to mend it but tired and soaking wet, gave up and wheeled his cycle for two hours, hoping to find somewhere to spend the night before darkness fell.

Eventually, he reached a deserted,

ramshackle farmhouse, boarded up except for the door which was ajar. He noticed a neglected, overgrown lake behind the building. Once inside, he could smell only damp and decay, the few remaining sticks of furniture being covered in mould. With no other choice, John tried to light a fire in the old fireplace, having found some dry wood. He went to fetch a bottle of paraffin from his saddle-bag. On returning to the farmhouse he was suddenly seized with fear when he noticed that across the hall there was a fresh trail of water, as though someone had just dragged a large, wet bundle across the dust-laden carpet, continuing into the living room, where John intended to light his fire, finishing on an old sofa where there was a pair of decaying pyjamas. Squirming, he threw these onto the floor and lit the fire which was suddenly blown out by a gust of wind.

Then he heard definite movement in the hall. Yet he found nothing there. Attempting to light the fire again, he heard it again. This time, he discovered the hall floor was soaking wet, actual water flowing towards him. Retreating back into the living room, it followed him. The current then made straight for the pair of decaying pyjamas on the floor which began to take on human form, as, like a dog, it shook off any signs of wetness.

Unable to take any more John fled the premises, ending up at the local bar where over a glass of cognac, he told the landlord his incredible story. Being offered a room for the night, the landlord assured him that his belongings would be safe left at the farmhouse because no-one dared go there after dark! Obviously, the place had got some sort of 'celebrity status'. Exhausted, and with help from the cognac, John slept well that night.

It was over breakfast next morning that the landlord showed John a collection of newspaper cuttings. Overcoming language difficulties, he learned that the farmhouse had been the home of an artist, Marc Baus. He had also been a collaborator during World War Two and had betrayed many French Resistance fighters to the Germans. In 1946, following his trial, he was sentenced to just two years' imprisonment and soon returned to his farmhouse, a broken man living in fear of reprisal. He had also lost family and friends.

One night, a crowd of people attacked the farmhouse. Fearing for his life, Baus escaped in his pyjamas and went missing. Two months later, he was pulled from the neglected, overgrown lake. His partly decomposed body was brought into the farmhouse and laid on the sofa in the living-room where a post mortem was carried out. The verdict was: 'Death by drowning either by accident or suicide'.

John also heard that in the year following Baus' death, two Frenchmen sheltering in the farmhouse during a thunderstorm had also fled after encountering the wet trail and the 'human-like' pyjamas.

Terror Beyond Belief

In 1940 following the dramatic fall of France, Nazi Germany quickly occupied the British Channel Islands near to the French coast, staying there until 1945. During this period a complex of tunnels on Jersey was hewn out by hand from solid rock by forced labour brought in from all over Europe. Many individuals, women and children included, died as a result of the terrible conditions they had to endure.

Today, Hohlgangsanlage 8 (HO8, as it is now known) at Les Charrieres Malorey, is a state-of-the-art, award-winning tourist attraction. Exhibits range widely from German radio equipment, weaponry, uniforms and medals, to the cells where prisoners were kept. Family snapshots left behind by German soldiers are still pinned to the walls where they were put originally. Contrasting experiences of the islanders are also depicted, besides stories of collaboration, captivity, siege, and finally, liberation; fascinating old newsreels show conditions on the island at the time.

'It moved me profoundly,' Lynne Bowker told me. A warm-hearted, sensitive woman in her mid-fifties from the Derbyshire Peak District, she and Tyler Byatte, her nine-year-old grandson, made a visit to the place several years ago. 'I could pick up all the cruelty and grief that had happened there. I could hardly breathe,' she added. 'At times, I just wanted to get out.'

HO8 had taken three years to construct as an armaments workshop and reinforced barracks. When the Allied Invasion of Europe seemed imminent, parts of it were adapted as a military hospital with accommodation for several hundred army personnel, complete with a well-equipped operating-theatre. In the end it was never used and is preserved as part of Jersey's history.

Considering what happened in places like HO8, a heavy, negative, even nauseous feeling is bound to linger, if not the actual ghosts themselves. Many tourists are keenly interested in such places and what insight they have to offer into the past by means of today's technology, including evocative lighting and sound effects, but not everyone is sensitive enough to 'pick up' the depth of atmosphere others can feel. Tyler's comment was 'I don't like it here, Gran!' while Lynne personally felt that the exhibits should have been on show elsewhere rather than in a place as 'dark' as HO8 itself. Yet possibly with 'auras' of their own, some of these objects might well take part of that atmosphere with them if removed.

In a similar context, the panelling from the room in Exeter House, now reconstructed in Derby Museum, is still said to reflect the despair of Bonnie Prince Charlie after his demoralising meeting with his military advisors in December, 1745. As we have already heard, this crucial confrontation marked an ignominious retreat and the loss of all the Prince's hopes of ever gaining the throne of England.

*   *   *

If life was pretty grim for the Channel Islanders, there was little comfort for the occupying German soldier. Sudden death by a sniper's bullet was not the only threat. Being discovered fraternising with 'the enemy' was another. When things started to go very badly for Hitler after the invasion of the Soviet Union in June 1941 (code-named 'Operation Barbarossa'), the terrible fear of being transferred to the Russian Front hung over all occupying military personnel on the Islands.

These factors would certainly have added to any prevailing emotional turmoil. On Guernsey not only the inhabitants but visitors unaware of its recent history have heard ghostly voices, shouting and cries of despair. Even phantom grey-uniformed German soldiers have been encountered along certain roads—indeed, young children have reported seeing them marching between Bourg and the old airport.

Phantom soldiers have also been sighted in certain houses, even in particular rooms. Perhaps this was where some used to be billeted. Someone who bought a house on the island after the war reported that family and friends who came to stay often saw a German soldier about the place. One of the bedrooms had a particularly dark, sinister atmosphere and the owner thought it could originally have been used by the soldier when he was alive. Perhaps he had received his dreaded transfer to the Russian Front and had left behind feelings of terror and resigned hopelessness. Or, as an alternative, did he choose to commit suicide rather than obey orders, his troubled spirit continuing to linger there?

As in Jersey, the Germans had tunnelling dug by slave labour into the hillside at La Vassalerie, a complex for ammunition storage and a military hospital. When filming there some years ago, the late Peter Sellers reported having been terrified, claiming he could almost touch the absolute fear still present in the atmosphere. This was an area the islanders themselves rarely visited at the time.

10
'FULL FATHOM FIVE . . . '

'Full fathom five thy father lies,
Of his bones are coral made;
Those are pearls that were his eyes,
Nothing of him that doth fade,
But doth suffer a sea-change
Into something rich and strange:
Sea-nymphs hourly ring his knell—
Hark! Now I hear them,
Ding-dong bell.'

Ariel's Song
William Shakespeare

Superstition has always been an integral part of life for those at sea. Indeed ships, always referred to by seamen as 'she', are either lucky or unlucky, so is it any wonder that we might find ourselves already 'halfway there' regarding spirited adventures on the high seas, where space is shared with weird atmospherics or a ghost or two? Here more than in other environment, death may call suddenly, whether during war or peace.

Victims not realising they are physically dead have even been known to appear, carrying on serving their ship's routine, or for the pure love of their job. Others, however, have found themselves 'stuck' inexplicably between life and death. There are ghosts of those who had connections to the sea and of those who actually went 'down to the sea in ships' who are also seen ashore.

Now a living museum and a mecca for tourists for over 400 years, Chatham Docks saw many of our Royal Navy warships built, from 'wooden-walls' to those of iron. Ship-builders, officers, ratings, admirals have passed through, often leaving behind something of themselves, and the place seems 'alive with the presence of the dead' (or perhaps undead?). From those in the old rope-house, where child labour was also once used in the spinning and laying of rope for rigging, to the vessels themselves they linger—the nameless and the famous. The spirit of Admiral Horatio Nelson has been seen where his ship *HMS Victory* was built on the instigation of the Prime Minister William Pitt in 1759. This ghost is of a much younger Nelson however, complete with his right eye (in which he was subsequently blinded at the siege of Calvi, also losing his right arm at Santa Cruz). It was as a lad that he joined the *Raisonable* as midshipman at Chatham Dockyard in 1770, under the command of his uncle, Maurice Suckling.

The more familiar thin, wispy figure of the great Admiral—minus his arm—has been spotted on bright spring mornings briskly striding across the quadrangle towards the former Admiralty Office in London. He once spent many happy and poignant times within this area in and around Somerset House.

*   *   *

It seems that the Royal Naval College at Greenwich hosts the phantom of the famous Admiral John Byng from almost a generation earlier. Footsteps have been heard in various corridors and domestic staff have been known to refuse to enter the most isolated rooms, saying they can detect something very strange about them. Byng was court marshalled and sentenced to be shot on the quarterdeck of *HMS Monarch* by firing squad on 17th March 1747, having failed to press home attacks on the French anchored just off British-held Minorca (though nowadays the opinion is that he was disposed of more for political reasons). Some of the college area was once used as a naval hospital and prior to his execution he was kept in one of the more isolated rooms. In ghostly form he has been seen trying to free himself not only from imprisonment but from the stigma of that terrible sentence imposed upon him.

Sir Francis Drake, an even earlier mariner, defeated the Spanish Armada in 1588 and subsequently became a folk-hero capable, in the public eye, of the most miraculous deeds. It was commonly believed he only had to pick up a wood-shaving and it would immediately be transformed into a fighting ship. Eight years later however, during a disastrous raiding expedition in the Caribbean, he lay dying and was ultimately buried at sea. A Devon man, he had given instructions that his drum should be returned to his home, Buckland Abbey near Plymouth, saying it would be heard when danger threatened our nation. It was suggested by some that Drake himself would also return during perilous times.

And indeed there came a time when Drake's Drum was actually heard. The Great War was over and the German fleet were to make their formal surrender on 21st November 1918 at Scapa Flow. The Royal Navy waited tensely as the first German battle-ships were sighted and: 'Prepare for action!' came the command, should the vanquished choose to unleash a final, defiant show of firing power.

It was aboard *HMS Royal Oak*, served mainly by Devon men, that the sound of a continuous series of drum-rolls was clearly heard by all, including Admiral Grant and their Captain Maclachan. At first it was assumed that someone was committing a serious breach of discipline—so much so that the ship was thoroughly searched twice. The drum-rolls still sounded until finally, still not satisfied, the Captain decided to make a check himself. Yet still those ominous drum rolls continued.

It was only in the early afternoon, when the entire German fleet had assembled and was completely surrounded by ships of the Royal Navy, that the drumming ceased. Many of those present believed that perhaps Drake had indeed risen from his watery grave, offering the sound of his drum a reassurance to his countrymen that the German Navy would show no resistance but would accept defeat with honour.

*   *   *

Sometimes as a result of an incident of great drama, ships have become ghosts or phantom vessels themselves. The image of the *Flying Dutchman,* doomed to sail the seas forever, has been seen by reliable eye witnesses over many years in several parts of the world; while Chaleur Bay, New Brunswick in Canada is said to be haunted by a British man-o'-war, sent there during the days of Queen Anne. Searches of old records have not revealed that any such ship was lost in the area during that early part of the 18th century—but the story continues.

In the mouth of the St Lawrence River there is the annual appearance of a ball of fire, which then assumes the shape of another old sailing ship. This is believed to be the *Packet Light,* whose fate is not known and can only be guessed at. Was she destroyed in flames by accident, or through an act of war?

It was certainly conflict that sealed the fate of *The Palatine.* For over 200 years the people of Block Island, New England claim to have seen an incandescent ship eerily plying the waters offshore at night. This is the phantom of the Dutch ship that was loaded with immigrants from Holland, bound for Philadelphia in 1752. As rations were low, the crew mutinied, murdering their captain and escaping in small boats, leaving the helpless passengers to fend for themselves as the ship ran aground on Block Island.

The luckless vessel met with a terrible welcome. *The Palatine* was pillaged by the islanders, who then set her on fire. Legend tells us that one madwoman refused to disembark as the current was about to sweep what remained of the burning ship back out to sea, and the sound of what seems a harsh, piercing laugh is said to be heard above the waves and the wind to this day. Is it a natural phenomenon—or is it the woman, still wailing aboard the phantom immigrant ship?

*   *   *

The following story was one vouched for by the late Lord Halifax. During the Great War a man we will call 'X', of magnetic charm and appearance, was the commander of one of a group of submarines operating from the south-east coast of England. Their remit was to patrol off the Dutch coast for 2–3 weeks at a time. By night they operated on the surface; by day underwater for fear of attack by German planes. From one such mission Commander 'X' and his crew never returned.

It was two months later that another submarine of the group broke surface with its periscope in that area, when the ship's officer saw someone ahead in the water, waving furiously. 'It's "X"!' he exclaimed, hardly believing his eyes. Having ordered the craft to fully surface, the crew immediately went out on deck with ropes to rescue the popular man. But when they looked he was nowhere to be seen. The officer was adamant that he had seen "X"—no-one could mistake his dynamic appearance.

Then suddenly two mines were ominously spotted straight ahead, bobbing in the water. Had the dead submarine commander appeared to warn his friends of the danger, so that they would not suffer the same fate he and his own crew had experienced?

170

Guardian Beyond Death—The Phantom Submariner

Powerful superstition is attached especially to ships that have had difficult launchings. For the ill-fated German U-Boat UB 65, on duty in the North Atlantic during the latter part of the Great War, things had even started to go wrong during its construction in 1916. Within a week of work commencing, a worker was killed outright by a falling girder, while another died later of his injuries. During the installation of the engines, three fitters were fatally overcome by fumes. Following its launch, a seaman was swept overboard and lost and due to a fault during its first dive, the vessel was unable to surface for twelve hours. Eventually reaching the surface the crew, gasping for breath, agreed gloomily that their charge must definitely be jinxed.

This seemed to be confirmed the next day. As torpedoes were being loaded one exploded, killing five seamen, including the second-in-command Lieutenant Richter, who was subsequently buried in the seaman's cemetery at Wilhelmshaven. But prior to the submarine leaving port, someone reported seeing him come aboard via the gangplank, walk to the bow, turn and face the coning tower, where he stood with folded arms. Another crew member who also saw the phantom was so terrified he jumped ship.

Surprisingly the UB-65's first mission proved successful; the crew sinking two merchant ships with torpedoes and destroying two others with gunfire. Then, despite being buffeted by rough seas in the English Channel with waves breaking over the vessel, a lookout reported seeing a figure in an officer's overcoat standing in the bow—and recognising him as the ghostly figure of Lieutenant Richter. Soon afterwards when UB-65 put into a Belgium port for a refit, her worried crew demanded transfers to other vessels. Word of the jinx had now spread throughout the German Navy and the Chief of German U-Boat Command, Admiral Schroeder, came himself to inspect the ship. Spending the night on board he slept well, subsequently dismissing any supernatural connection as rubbish.

Yet might this have been because someone had already asked a Lutheran pastor to come and perform an exorcism? And was it also due to the pastor's intervention that the following two missions proved relatively uneventful? Certainly the captain, Commander Gustav Schelle, threatened anyone with severe punishment if they so much as mentioned ghosts.

*   *   *

Life on board an early submarine like UB-65 was cramped, hot, very smelly, with no privacy for the individual. Stacked close to live torpedoes, even bunks were shared with those comrades on different shifts. As the war continued, nerves would become more frayed as German U-Boat losses increased, for the crews knew full well that they only had a fifty-fifty chance of survival.

In May 1918, off the coast of Spain, another sighting of Lieutenant Richter's ghost drove a torpedo crewman into such complete insanity that he threw himself overboard. And this in turn seemed to trigger off a new set of tragedies. A petty officer was swept away by heavy seas; the chief engineer fell, breaking his leg. Soon afterwards another crew member died of injuries sustained after the vessel had been attacked by depth-charges from Allied ships on the surface. And after briefly putting into port in June 1918, UB-65 set out on what was to be her final voyage.

On July 10th the commander of a United States submarine, Lieutenant Forster, closed in on a German submarine that appeared to be listing heavily off the southern coast of Ireland. Suspecting a possible trap, he cautiously manoeuvred his vessel round it, preparing to launch a torpedo. Before he could fire however, there was a massive explosion as UB-65 was transformed into an inferno of fire and smoke. The stricken vessel then reared up, finally sinking into the Atlantic. The Americans moved in to investigate but all that was left was debris and there were no apparent human remains. According to one source, however, Lieutenant Forster thought for a fleeting moment that he caught sight of someone positioned in the bow of the stricken submarine immediately before it went down—a man wearing a German officer's overcoat, standing with folded arms.

The explosion has remained a mystery ever since although, at the time, Lieutenant Forster wondered if there had been another German submarine close by. Perhaps the jinxed UB-65 had been there as a decoy, and was accidentally hit by a torpedo intended for the American submarine.

In July, 1968 Sven Morgens-Larsen with his wife June and family, was aboard his yacht in the same area. Enjoying supper on deck early one evening, they heard a muffled explosion underwater and the sea began to swell at a spot a few yards away. Then a conning tower suddenly broke surface, followed by the bows of a vintage German submarine. To the intense surprise of everyone, there was clearly visible a figure in a naval overcoat, standing in the bow with folded arms. Then he disappeared, being followed just as suddenly by the submarine itself in a cloud of vapour. Astutely, however, Morgens-Larsen had had time to note through his binoculars that her markings, which he later reported, included the figures 6 and 5.

By way of subsequent research, he was convinced that what the group had seen had been the spectre of UB-65. Its appearance at precisely 6.30pm on 10th July, 1968 coincided with the exact position where she had met her end 50 years before, on 10th July, 1918. It is intriguing to wonder whether this phantom vessel would have surfaced had the Morgens-Larsen family not been there to witness it

Phantoms of a Queen

Even luxury liners may be called into war service. For over thirty years the British *Queen Mary* and her sister ship *Queen Elizabeth* crossed the North Atlantic, carrying passengers between Europe and North America. This was interrupted by World War Two when she was commandeered as a troopship, before resuming her luxury status once more. Retired in 1967, the once British flagship of the Cunard White Star Line (now moored at Long Beach Harbour, California) was converted into an exclusive hotel and resort which was opened in 1972. Accommodation offered ranged from small cabins to large state rooms.

Inevitably, during those long years at sea

she had many comings and goings, including the deaths of some passengers. Phantoms of stowaways who had died on board have been seen in the engine room, whilst during the 1960s a crew member was crushed to death by a falling metal door. Here, too, a spectral bearded man in overalls has been spotted. The swimming-pool in the first-class section, now kept only half-full, is haunted by two ghostly children. A ghostly blonde woman has also been seen swimming around. On emerging, she leaves a set of wet footprints which, like her, just disappear. Equally as strange, it is said that there is a vortex through which it is possible to enter other dimensions, situated beneath a revolving door that was once used as an entrance to the swimming-pool.

And we must not forget that a ship such as the *Queen Mary* retains the spirits of many pets as well as those of some former passengers. For example in the early hours of the morning the anguished howls of an Irish setter are sometimes heard, his owner having died years ago in his sleep on board—while desperate cries of a different kind have been heard down in the bows.

It was on October 2nd 1942, while bringing American troops to England escorted by the British destroyer *HMS Corocoa* as protection against the threat of German submarines that a terrible tragedy occurred. The two captains somehow misunderstood each other, with the result that there was a serious collision. The *Queen Mary* received a tear in her bow, but the *Corocoa* was sliced in two by the huge liner and sank within five minutes. 338 lives were lost, and none of her crew could be rescued due to the larger ship having orders not to stop, or even slow down, for fear of attack by German U-boats.

It was during the liner's refit as a hotel that John Smith, the ship's engineer, regularly inspected the hull when she was first moored at Long Beach to check that no water was being taken on. Everything seemed fine, although every time he approached the bow of the ship he thought he heard not only the sound of rushing water but also the desperate cries of men about to drown. There was still no sign of any water coming in, and knowing he had been thorough with every inspection, Smith was also well aware that all ships tended to emit structural creaks and groans, especially older vessels. It was only later that he learned about the fatal tragedy in the autumn of 1942.

*   *   *

The *USS Lexington,* a World War Two aircraft carrier is now a museum based on dry land in Corpus Christi, Texas. Over thirty men died on board during her years of active service, so the ship has its fair quota of ghost stories. Volunteer members of staff have often been aware of someone walking ahead of them along the many passages out-of-bounds to visitors. Anyone trying to apprehend the figure finds it simply disappears. One of the most well known presences is that of a tall, blond, blue-eyed young sailor in a white uniform. He moves amiably about the ship, talking, chatting to visitors and giving them relevant information, yet when questioned about this charming young man, the staff are obliged to explain that there was actually no-one of that description on board!

The *USS Hornet*, the eighth naval vessel to carry that name, is claimed to be the most haunted warship in the American Navy. During World War Two she saw heavy action in the South Pacific against Japanese forces in Iwo Jima, Saipon, Tinian, the Philippines and Okinawa, eventually being awarded 9 battle stars for her services. In 1969, via the news media, the whole world saw her recover the Apollo 11 astronauts on their return from the moon. The following year she was decommissioned and declared an historical landmark at the former naval air station in Alameda, California.

She has been the focus of many television programmes, which have revealed that during her active life between 1943 and 1970 an estimated 300 plus personnel died on board by way of combat or accident. Ghostly footsteps and disembodied voices have frequently been heard; spectral crewmen and officers in khaki descending ladders have been witnessed, powerful winds have whistled through enclosed areas, while sophisticated electrical equipment has mysteriously been switched on and off. One of the phantoms often seen is that of Admiral Joseph James Clark, her former captain, who died in 1970. Of Cherokee descent, he was the first Native American to graduate from the Annapolis U.S. Naval Academy in Maryland in 1917. Like many other ghosts on board *USS Hornet*, he has been seen to be friendly, with a great sense of humour!

That sense of humour was a very valued commodity in wartime, one veteran of the British Merchant Fleet recently told me. Having served in the Mediterranean as well as on the convoys to Russia, he was emphatic that 'as well as the dangers, there were plenty of laughs'. There had to be in order to survive.

11
THOSE MAGNIFICENT GHOSTS . . .

'They were my companions many a year,
A portion of my mind and life, as it were,
And now their breathless faces seem to look
Out of some old picture-book . . . '

In memory of Major Robert Gregory
W.B. Yeats

Since the earliest days of aviation there was a strong romanticism, a fascinating mystique around 'those magnificent men in their flying-machines'. Necessarily young, forward-looking and with an attitude of devil-may-care, these were the men who assumed the roles of fighter pilot or crew member of a bomber, their bravery, wits and cunning tested to the full. Where the 'discourtesy of death' has occurred it appears that some might not wish to be regarded as part of the past, and as with other cases we have already encountered, there are those who do not realise they are actually dead.

Exposed and abandoned airfields, once hubs of massive wartime activity, can have atmospheres now of cold eeriness. Amid the duties, personal celebrations and tragedies that occurred in such places, is it no surprise that phantom airmen and other people long dead still haunt old conning towers, rusted Nissen-huts and hangars that rattle ominously in the wind.

The airfield at Montrose on the coast of Scotland was first used by the Royal Flying Corps in 1913. By the outbreak of war the following year it was a training centre for pilots. Everyone became aware of the Montrose ghost, the phantom figure of an airman seen around the living quarters and other places by a number of staff. It was believed to be the spectre of Lieutenant Desmond Arthur, killed in May 1913 when his aircraft crashed on take-off. Seemingly a man who was not popular with ground crew or fellow trainee pilots, he claimed as he lay dying that his machine had been tampered with. This is such a fine ghostly yarn that the actual facts do not seem to matter—some believe the story really occurred during World War Two.

When Lord Balfour heard this tale back in the Great War, he thought the ghost was actually that of another trainee pilot who crashed during his first solo flight, having told his instructor beforehand that he felt unready to face the challenge. The night after his death, the instructor awoke and saw his young student's phantom standing by the bed wearing blood-stained flying-kit before it disappeared. Panic-stricken, the instructor next day demanded a post elsewhere, and a new flying instructor took his place. He also witnessed the appearance of the blood-stained phantom in his room. Soon, another replacement instructor experienced the same thing, so the commanding officer had the room sealed off.

Other people believed the spectre was that of the pilot of a Sopwith Camel which disappeared over the Scottish moors. It was only found years later, so the story goes, with the skeleton of the pilot still on board. But whoever the ghost actually was, there is no doubt that he thought himself still to be alive.

Flying Bravely into History

It was one day in April 1916, on a small airfield behind the front lines in France that members of the Royal Flying Corps stared agog as a single-seater Neuport fighter suddenly came spluttering through the clouds, doing all sorts of wild aerobatics. They identified the pilot as Lieutenant Peretti of the Cignone Escadrille. His plane, heavily peppered with bullet-holes, came into land with everyone realising it was going far too fast. Yet somehow, it managed a good three-point landing.

It seemed unable to stop, and as they all ran towards the stricken machine it suddenly turned over. Pulling him out of the wreckage, they discovered that Lieutenant Peretti was dead—but this was not due to the crash. He had been shot right through the head and death would have been immediate. So had Peretti flown back to base, not knowing he was actually dead? Or had the plane found its own way back, piloted by forces we do not understand, in order that he could have a known, final resting-place?

During World War Two, another story involved 'Fly-boy Willie'. As a crew-member of a Wellington bomber, he took off from the RAF base at Lindhulme in South Yorkshire on a raiding mission over Germany in 1944. The plane was severely damaged and did not quite make it home, but instead crashed into a bog between Doncaster and the River Humber killing all its crew. Despite this, Willie's former commanding officer said that he and other personnel often heard him clumping upstairs in his flying boots and then coming down again.

'My son once actually saw and spoke to him,' he maintained. 'Willie was wearing his full flying-kit.'

The airfield at East Kirkby near Horncastle, Lincolnshire was used as an American bomber base. A pilot thus far from home was killed when his B17 crashed nearby, and his ghostly figure has been seen walking towards the control tower, his shredded parachute dragging behind him. At Burtonwood near

Warrington, Cheshire, there was another American airbase. Bailing out from his plummeting aircraft, one young pilot caught his head on the cockpit canopy and his headless ghost has been sighted in the vicinity ever since. At night at East Cowes on the Isle of Wight, witnesses claim to have seen another headless pilot drift down to earth by parachute—a security dog that once saw the apparition went so berserk it never recovered and had to be put down. And ever since 1941, at the airfield at Hawarden near to Chester, the phantom figure of an RAF sergeant has lingered at the spot where his fighter plane exploded in a ball of flame.

*   *   *

Particularly in war, a kind of bonding can develop between individual airmen and the planes they fly, until the demise of one or the other or both. Such bonding may seem so powerful it can transcend even death.

A solitary Spitfire has been seen to fly low at very high speed over Biggin Hill, the famous Battle of Britain airfield in Kent. Although not always visible, it screams in to land with the phantom pilot sometimes signalling his return with a spectacular victory roll. Another interesting case is connected with the Aerospace Museum at RAF Cosford in Shropshire. Here a phantom airman dressed in

184

air force blue and with a white polo-necked sweater appears whenever staff are working on one post-war Lincoln Bomber in particular—No.RF398. Incredibly, so it is said, he even helps them with the job.

He was thought at one time to be the ghost of a doomed Spitfire pilot, his plane having been restored and housed at the museum. Eventually it was dispatched elsewhere but the spirit airman remained, turning his attention not only to the well-being of the Lincoln Bomber but also to its 'carers'. During one particularly cold winter, it was noticeable that the interior always felt warm and cosy to work in. On another occasion when someone fell backwards off the fuselage, crashing to the floor, he miraculously sustained no injuries. With 'Fred' around, there always seems to be a sense of wellbeing. Tasks get done quickly. John Small, an ex-RAF fitter, has said that rewiring through the Bomber's wings was normally a long job, but it was completed in two days.

It is now thought that 'Fred' was more likely to have been the pilot of a plane that crashed nearby during the 1940s, with no survivors. Yet he could also be the spirit of an aero engineer who committed suicide in the late 1940s, when the bomber he had been responsible for crashed, killing everyone on board. Pieces of the wreckage were actually brought into the hangar at Cosford. Yet since the site was first opened just prior to World War Two, many repair and maintenance teams have passed through its important Maintenance Unit over the years. Staff feel convinced that 'Fred' is keen to get the Lincoln Bomber in working order again so that he might take off once more.

Staff on the evening shift at a Thurmaston (Leicestershire) food factory were more than puzzled when they saw the figure of someone in a flying-suit with a fur collar, who seemed to be hanging around at their place of work. A clairvoyant who was called in believed it was the ghost of a pilot or crew-member of a World War Two plane. There had once been a scrap yard where the factory stood and it is thought that the remains of his crashed plane were brought there. Did his ghostly self arrive with it, or did he come later and is still checking it out?

Haunted Bombers—and Bogs

The now abandoned World War Two airfield at Bottesford, also in Leicestershire, still echoes to the sound of a low-flying bomber while eerie, unidentified lights have been seen over the derelict control tower. What remains of the medieval, war-ravaged Coventry Cathedral (next to the present Cathedral), has also reverberated to the drone of German aircraft flying over, as they did in the early 1940s. At Hawkinge near Folkstone, a phantom German flying-bomb has been heard droning across the clear sky over 60 years since hostilities ceased.

I have heard it rumoured (although I have been unable to come across conclusive information) that one of the lakes beneath the shadow of Snowdon, in North Wales, hosts wreckage of enemy planes from World War Two, and its shore still echoes to the desperate calls of ghostly German voices. We can assume that the planes and their crews perished when they crashed into the mountains, following bombing missions over Liverpool. Even in summer, thick mist can suddenly descend over the area without warning.

This can also happen in the Peak District, a mystical, highly-charged area, spread over parts of South Yorkshire, Derbyshire and Staffordshire. Many experts including journalist/investigators David Clarke and Jenny Randles agree that there is something very strange and powerful at work there. Not only renowned for its ancient earth spirits, ghosts, inexplicable lights and UFO activities, the Peak District might also boast the highest number of ghost planes and phantom airmen than in any other part of the British Isles. Many such planes that came to grief there, with fatal consequences for their crews, during and just after World War Two, would have taken off from emotionally-charged airfields anyway, with ghosts of many airmen already wandering around.

The moors of Howdon and Bolsterstone, with their desolate peat bogs, are said to be resting grounds for about 300 airmen and civilian pilots. But do they all rest peacefully? Where crashes have occurred, many searches have been abandoned, due to deteriorating weather conditions and the inhospitable terrain. Strangely, this has been happening in the wider area for over seventy years and is still happening.

Wreckage of planes can still be found in the more remote parts of the Peak District, particularly in the Longdendale Valley, Derbyshire where ghost planes have been sighted many times, re-enacting their fatal few moments prior to crashing. Some appear to soar into the sky, then disappear. Others fly in very low, some witnesses even 'ducking' as the aircraft passes overhead, propellers turning, sometimes silently. Others come with engines roaring.

In May 1945, a Lancaster Bomber, of 408 Squadron and its Canadian crew took off from RAF Linton-on-Ouse. Approaching the Peak District, parts of which rise to a height of 2,000 feet, the pilot lost his bearings due to the mist, fog and fading light and crashed into Jane's Thorn, on Bleaklow. Hardly two months later, an American Dakota crashed in almost the same spot, all 27 members of the crew being killed. These two planes have been seen in ghostly form not only by local people, but also by visitors to the area.

It was whilst out with his dog Ben, a golden retriever, one day in April 1994 that Tony Ingle, a retired postman from Chesterfield had an experience of a lifetime. On a short break at Hope, he was walking near to where both the Lancaster bomber and Dakota had crashed all those years before. Suddenly he was aware of a large prop-powered plane coming in low—actually casting a shadow as it passed silently overhead. It then tried to turn, banking steeply, and seemed to disappear over the brow of a nearby hill. With Ben, Tony rushed to the top, expecting to see masses of wreckage. Instead there was nothing.

Later he identified the plane as a Dakota, though investigation revealed that the sole RAF Dakota flying that day was over 150 miles away. Had Tony actually encountered the aircraft that crashed there in 1945—or rather, its ghostly equivalent? He was to return to the site several times afterwards, but saw nothing, although his dog Ben refused to go near the place.

It was in 1948 that an American B-29 Superfortress also lost its bearings in similar circumstances and crashed high up into Bleaklow. Pieces of wreckage can still be seen in the peat bogs.

Silent Phantoms Still Walk

At the first full moon of spring, another Lancaster bomber in phantom form is seen to skim the waters of Ladybower reservoir then disappear. Though it is not connected to the famous 617 Squadron, it continues to patrol the area where the 'Dam Busters' practiced their dangerous manoeuvres, flying low over the nearby dams of Howdon and Derwent reservoirs prior to successfully attacking the Mohne and Eder dams in Germany during 1943, with the famous 'bouncing bomb'. Though they risked their necks on these essential sorties before the 'real thing', it seems there were no accidents, and the bomber that became the Ladybower ghost plane crashed close by during the early months of 1945, killing its mainly Australian crew.

Convinced they have witnessed actual crashes people have sometimes called out the rescue services, though in all cases, after hours of searching they have given up, convinced that there was nothing to be found. Coupled with the sighting of ghost planes, inevitably there have been encounters with what witnesses believe to be phantom airmen. One wet and misty morning, a hiker saw a ghostly figure emerge from Derwent reservoir, wearing a flying-coat with what seemed like a fur collar. The phantom then made for a nearby wood and disappeared. The hiker was convinced it was from the World War Two era, although he did say that the figure appeared to be out of proportion with the surroundings— as though it was something being projected onto some sort of screen. He said that the experience gave him a very weird feeling.

As a schoolboy Gerald Scarratt, a local historian, remembered the B-29 crash high up on Bleaklow in 1948 and years later, took his son up to see the wreckage. It was raining and something caught his eye in the wet soil. Picking it up, he thought it was a small washer but when it was cleaned up, Gerald found it was actually a gold ring engraved with the letters LPT, the initials of the pilot Langdon P. Tanner. This discovery gained some publicity and as a result Gerald was soon visiting the site again, this time accompanied by a group of plane enthusiasts. As he bent down to show them the spot where the ring had been found, his audience suddenly backed away some twenty yards. They explained that a ghostly figure of someone in flying kit had been standing right behind him. The group thanked him for bringing them up to Bleaklow, but they decided they were off home—quick!

*   *   *

Souvenir hunting has been very much discouraged, whether it be small objects or larger pieces of debris. And this respect for the dead has been reinforced by other laws than those which are man-made. A farmer went up onto Sykes Moor, near Glossop where an RAF Blenheim had crashed back in 1939, looking for material he might adapt for his own agricultural machinery, which he stored in one of the barns. One day, when he and his son were engaged on their scavenging, they watched horror-stricken as the whole structure began to shake so violently they thought it was about to fall down. Immediately they decided to return everything they had taken from Sykes Moor!

A former railwayman, John Davies and a friend, who both lived in Longdendale Valley, took pieces from the same plane. Then one night, aghast, they heard what they thought was the sound of a huge animal, like a large cat, padding and sniffing around the garage where the pieces of debris were kept. John's father, thinking it was some ghostly spirit, told him to take the pieces 'straight off back' to where they belonged. They were duly returned to the moors and buried.

In another case a man was given a propeller from the same plane only for him to become convinced it was responsible for a tragic series of misfortunes that hit himself and his family a year later. He was glad to get rid of it, and after he had returned it to its original site, fortune began to go a lot better for him.

Near the Grains-in-Water area of Bleaklow the atmosphere is very strange, the beautiful scenery luring many walkers into the area. Some have, indeed, experienced inexplicable encounters. Two young men in pursuit of the remains of a World War Two aircraft once found themselves being pursued on what seemed an ordinary, beautiful, sunny day when with no warning, a patch of mist suddenly descended and in its midst they saw some elemental presence in giant human form, making straight for them. Like the birds and the sheep nearby, the men just panicked and cleared off as fast as possible, tumbling down the steep slopes as they went.

Lower down the mist gave way to the sun again and having calmed and gained their breath, they felt as though they had just returned from a sinister world very distant from their own. Had they encountered some sort of paranormal custodian of the planes that had been wrecked on those lonely heights? It might well seem so, but they had actually come face-to-face with what is known in the Peak District as the Dark Lad or T'Owd Lad, a horned man—or spirit—who is said to haunt the whole of the wide area with its stone circles, cairns and barrows; an area that fatefully acknowledges the ways of the ancient gods, still demanding their sacrificial rites.

12
MARCHING ON

'War's annals will cloud into night
Ere their story die.'

In Time of 'The Breaking of Nations'
Thomas Hardy

Wars and challenging times come and go each leaving behind their own mark on civilisation. How long each may last does not seem to be all that important. A sudden stabbing or well-aimed sniper's bullet can as well boost an already highly-charged atmosphere as—shall we say—the Battle of Culloden of 1746 (duration of approximately one hour) or the near 400 years' Roman Occupation of Great Britain. Each of these events and many others regarded as pivotal are thus assured of their prominent place in history. Yet our awareness of many others—even those which were considered as pivotal in their own time—has tended to become air-brushed into near oblivion, even though they too, may resound with psychic echoes and still go marching on.

While 1812 saw Napoleon causing havoc in Europe, for example, war was also being fought between the USA and Great Britain and its colonies—especially Canada. Fort Erie,

194

Ontario, built shortly after the French and Indian War was settled by the Treaty of Paris in 1763, had been associated with a series of unpleasant apparitions down the years, including that of a man with missing hands and another with no head. During the War of 1812, an American corporal was shaving his sergeant with a cut-throat razor when a British cannon-ball struck, leaving the corporal minus his hands and the sergeant without his head. To substantiate this story, the gruesome remains of a headless man were later found, together with an arm with no hand, during excavations at the fort.

During the same war, at Niagara-on-the-Lake, Ontario, a British Captain Swayze sought refuge in the cellars of the Old Angel Inn, in a bid to escape from some American soldiers. As they approached, he tried hiding in a barrel, but was too late as they burst in, Swayze being killed by a thrust from a bayonet. During the American retreat shortly afterwards, the Inn was set alight and destroyed, only to be rebuilt in 1815.

From the 1820s onwards, however, a number of strange happenings were reported. These included the appearance of smartly-dressed men and women, ghostly footsteps and hearty male laughter heard in the dining-room besides fife and drum music being played in an upstairs bedroom. Could some of these manifestations have been 'inherited' from the original Old Angel Inn which had stood on the same site? It is, after all, not an uncommon occurrence. The clue could have been the appearance of a red-coated man seen in the mirror of the then new ladies' room, next to the cellars where Captain Swayze had met his death.

In February 1836, during the Texan War of Independence, and in rebellion against Mexico's self-appointed dictator General Santa Anna, it was Colonel William B. Travis who arrived with almost 200 Texan volunteers to help those already inside the Alamo. This fort, once the Mission of San Antonio de Valero, San Antonio, Texas was established in 1718 as one of a series of Catholic missions by Spanish Franciscan monks in their crusade to convert the native American Indians to Christianity.

Although they managed to hold on for thirteen days the brave, determined Texans were finally defeated by an equally determined Mexican Army, which made this one of the most tragic sieges in the history of the United States. It not only witnessed the deaths of legendary figures like William B. Travis himself, Jim Bowie and Davy Crockett, but those of every other defender inside the fort. Despite the tragedy, they had managed to slow down the progress of the Mexican Army, giving time for their fellow comrades to assemble more supplies of arms in readiness for their later challenge at San Jacinto. This campaign the Texans won, thus ending the war. Ever since, visitors to Alamo have sensed its eerie atmosphere, while some have seen the ghosts of injured and disfigured men walking or staggering through the walls of the fort. Uncanny screams have been heard at night. Some people even claim to have encountered the ghosts of William B. Travis and Jim Bowie while others have spotted phantom horsemen riding by.

One of the last battles of the Mexican-American War took place in 1847 at San Pasqual in California. Despite the bitter savagery, there were also acts of heroism and bravery on both sides. But the outcome was questionable, indecisive, and subject to occasional debate even to this day, despite the conflict being half-forgotten. And yet, according to Richard Senate, an American parapsychologist there remain 'deep psychic scars' and 'many accounts exist of ghosts wandering the site.' At night, on each anniversary of the Battle of San Pasqual—6th December—it is said that over both the battlefield and the nearby mass grave where the dead from both sides are buried, an icy wind always blows. People have also heard eerie cries way down the canyon, besides witnessing phantom American and Mexican soldiers locked in eternal combat.

By contrast, two phantom armies not often seen now—and believed to have almost 'run out of energy' derived their 'immortality' from action seen on 17th May 1828, during the Greek War of Independence. This was when a company of 900 Turkish soldiers attacked almost 400 Greeks, near the Venetian fortress of Frangocastello on the coast of Crete. The Greeks being totally slaughtered, reports soon gathered pace that both spectral armies appeared at dawn on 17th May, the anniversary of this, another half-forgotten battle.

> *'The spirit world around this world of sense*
> *Floats like an atmosphere, and everywhere*
> *Wafts through those earthly mists and*
> *   vapours dense*
> *A vital breath of more ethereal air.'*

Henry Wadsworth Longfellow

* * *

Many scientists now accept that ghosts or spirits could well be a perfectly natural phenomenon. After all, they have been with us for such a long time and the source of many incredible and persistent stories since the dawning of various civilisations. For many people there has always been more to life beyond the physical—whether entailing belief in one or more of the various gods, or spirits of ancestors, some of which as we know have appeared as heroes on the battlefield.

By contrast there are those people who are denying themselves a wonderfully 'boundless reality'—an attitude which would perhaps still cling stubbornly to the theory that the Earth was flat. They could even be afraid—not so much of the paranormal but simply because it represents something beyond their control.

Where traumatic happenings like battles have taken place evidence suggests that energies *can* linger, perhaps imbedded in the atmosphere for many years afterwards. As we know, given the right set of conditions such energies may result in a replay or at least the re-creating of an original feeling of terror and futility. Through ways we still do not understand—and do we really *want* to know the answers to all the mysteries of life and death?—these phenomena could be triggered by the presence of a person, or persons who may be naturally attuned to psychic activity— thus completing the 'circuit', as it were— whether they may be aware of their gift or not.

Some thirty years ago when my wife Dilys was crossing the North Sea on her way to Sweden she awoke in her cabin during the night feeling wretchedly ill, distressed and upset for what, she thought, was no apparent reason. It was certainly not seasickness—for at that moment the ship's engines had actually, inexplicably stopped. Eventually, her intense discomfort gradually subsided. It was only later that she learned that at the time of her distress, the ship had been in the area where the Battle of Jutland, one of the most savage naval conflicts of World War One, had taken place.

This happened long before she realised that she was psychic, but asked whether she would be just as upset if she were to repeat the same trip today, Dilys told me that having been able to develop her psychic gifts over a number of years since, she would almost certainly still 'pick up' on the intense tragedy, but would now be better equipped to cope with the situation.

Incidentally, in the years before she began her psychic work she also experienced a similar situation when visiting the battlefields of Northern France.

'It was most embarrassing, because I could not help myself, as the bus was taking us to Ypres, tears were running down my face and I could not stop them. The impression of terrible sadness and tragedy was almost unbearable.'

*   *   *

Our understanding of time, where the present may be regarded as a vehicle roller-coasting down a straight line with all of us on board, could be seriously challenged by our concept of the so-called 'paranormal'. As we are aware ghosts, although their behaviour tends to be well within the boundaries of human nature and whether civilian or military, seem to ignore the settings in which they appear as the places are today. They may walk along a gravel path where there is now grass, move through walls where doors no longer exist, sit on seats that are no longer there or (tantalisingly!) read or refer to manuscripts long since been destroyed or missing.

Our encounters with ghosts tend to happen quite unexpectedly, like the afternoon breeze parting filmy curtains which drape an open window. We may glimpse the familiar garden outside or familiar street below—or for a split second 'go back' in time, to catch two soldiers from a bygone era involved in a desperate sword-fight against the setting of a courtyard or woodland of which we have no previous knowledge, the scene that was there long before the homes, gardens or streets of today were even contemplated.

Then, as we have mentioned there are also examples of interaction between living people and those of long ago, like the case of Lord Percival Durand and his friends who encountered the crusty Flavius Mantus, a

Roman Custos while picnicking near to Wroxham on the Norfolk Broads in 1829; or the Reverend Thomas Penston when he met up with the same spirit in 1709; and the experience that Benjamin Curtis and his two friends claimed to have undergone while swimming in the same area approximately a century before that.

Another example is Maurice Cottham, a guide at St. Peter's Church, Monkwearmouth, who experienced a 'fatal' knife-thrust deep into his chest—compliments of a warrior possibly from late Anglo-Saxon times.

*   *   *

So by our current understanding of the fundamental laws of nature there might be less scope in believing that time itself simply keeps marching on. It could be that time even stops, bends in a curve or even moves backwards. Probably every one of us has been challenged by the inexplicable one way or another, even if superficially, having felt perhaps just the sensation that time can pass at varying speeds and intensities.

As part of the human experience, even if briefly (I know I have mentioned this before) those old yet persistent atmospheres may also be sensed not only where there has been human suffering but that of animals—a barn, for example, which might have been the setting for the slaughter of farm animals in the past or even the terror of old or injured war-horses, their final, agonised neighings can still be heard under certain conditions even though their physical remains are no longer there.

So do we, time-wise, go back to them all? Or do their images—whether by sight, sound or smell (or by all three)—come to us? Or where any kind of hauntings occur (human or animal) are they spirits, for some reason or another 'stuck' between their former earth-life and the ultimate Light?

In his book *Lychgate—The Entrance to the Path*, Air Chief Marshal Lord Hugh Dowding, a dedicated member of the Spiritualist Church, in charge of the RAF in those crucial days during the Battle of Britain in 1940 actually mentioned psychics who engaged in 'rescue work'—by being able to help those souls trapped on other planes to finally move on, particularly those of soldiers, seamen and airmen who find themselves stranded, not realising that they have left their physical bodies. He later expressed his belief that his men had been protected by higher powers (in spite of inevitable losses) throughout the air Battle of Britain. This belief was very much shared by a number of his fellow-RAF personnel and US air-crews throughout World War Two.

But what of those individuals killed in action who appear to members of their family maybe within seconds, minutes or hours of their dying, to indicate that, although they have departed from this life they are happy, often relieved to have left the scenes of conflict? There are many examples recorded, particularly from the time of the First World War as we have learned. There has even been the suggestion that such 'crisis apparitions' as they are called, might indicate that the transition from the 'life state' to that of death (or passing to the Light) might, in many cases, not be as sudden as is often assumed; that perhaps there are several transitional stages, so that during one or more, the apparition of the 'dying' soldier—if he so wishes—appears to be very much alive in the eyes of loved ones before, in the majority of instances, he 'moves on.'

Or could it be a matter of some altered state of consciousness being involved, whereby under crisis conditions, the 'dying' person in question is able by choice, to cause himself to spontaneously self-project or go out-of-body? This, as we know, does not *necessarily* mean that the person who appears as a crisis apparition is 'dead'. Perhaps at that particular moment he was in great danger—a moment of high drama—if not connected to the military, then involved in some other crisis—road or rail disaster, climbing or air accident, where he had managed to survive very much against the odds.

Each year on Remembrance Sunday, on or near 11th November, people gather together at the Cenotaph in London and in cities, towns and villages throughout the country and in many other lands. Thinking of fiancés, husbands, fathers, sons and daughters, uncles, nephews, nieces and old comrades who fell by the hand of conflict, many of those attending often remark that although deeply moved by the Service, they have felt deeply comforted that their lost ones, for just a few minutes, are actually there with them.

Perhaps that is true, their spirits empowered by the collective emotional energy of those wanting to remember and respecting them. After all, no-one has proved that there is no after-life. Perhaps not only do our ghostly soldiers continue to progress, but we ourselves will some day join them to go marching on together.

THANKS

I would like to thank everyone who has shared their experiences of 'ghosts at war' with me— also those who took the trouble to record their impressions of paranormal occurrences in previous years and previous centuries.

Without being able to draw on past records (whether recorded on parchment, paper or passed on verbally to their descendents) we would never know of the ghostly visitations inspired by ancient conflict.

I am also grateful to the authors of the many books I have consulted on this subject.

Paul Gater